S0-AKS-711

Let's Ride

Let's Ride

Carol Green

octopus

Contents

First published 1979 by Octopus Books Limited
59 Grosvenor Street, London W1

ISBN 0 7064 0735 2

© 1979 Octopus Books Limited

Designed by Astrid Publishing Consultants

Produced by Mandarin Publishers Limited,
22A Westlands Road, Quarry Bay, Hong Kong

Printed in Singapore

Foreword

Everybody basically rides for their own enjoyment and relaxation. "Let's Ride" will give the complete beginner an insight into what is involved in riding and keeping a horse or pony, and to the person who has already started, a better understanding of what it is they are trying to do.

After reading "Let's Ride", the beginner will have an excellent grounding in the fundamentals of horsemanship. This, combined with a good instructor, will enable the first horse or pony to be faced with confidence.

This book will be of interest to those who have already started to ride in that it may well help them to understand what they have been doing, or trying to do. It also gives them some useful advice on how they can best progress and enjoy their riding even more.

I wish all those who read this book and decide to start with a pony every success and happiness with their riding and hope they get as much enjoyment out of it as myself. I should perhaps warn them though that it is not as easy as it looks, but the sense of achievement is well worth some of the thrills and spills.

Chapter 1

Let's go riding

Riding and looking after horses is a year-round sport that is enjoyed by all ages. You do not have to be particularly talented or wealthy to enjoy them. You need not even wish to ride to take part. You may simply enjoy watching horse shows on television, or you may be very keen and hope to become a three-day event rider, or even be on television.

If you do want to learn to ride you will be happiest and safest at a riding school. Here an experienced instructor will see that you start on a suitable pony so that you can gain skill and confidence.

When choosing a school, look for one with a neat and tidy yard and well cared for and healthy looking animals. If they take proper care of the ponies it is to be hoped they will take care of you. Most national horse societies publish booklets recommending suitable schools and these are good guides too.

Once you have learned to ride reasonably well much pleasure may be gained by hacking. Many people find it very relaxing and a really lovely way to see the countryside, enjoy the good fresh air and get some exercise.

You may find that you want to get really involved with horses and perhaps even own a horse or pony of your own. You can spend many hours learning about horse management. The care of the horse through all seasons is a vast subject. The best way to start learning is to offer to help a friend who has a pony or to help out at the local stables as an assistant groom. Always stay alert and you will learn a great deal about the practical handling of horses. Also read as much as you can about horse management.

For most people under the age of 20, Pony Clubs are excellent. By being a member of a Pony Club you are able to share your hobby with other people, attend lectures, demonstrations and rallies and work for efficiency tests. Adults may join riding clubs which are run on similar lines to pony clubs so you are able to meet people who share interests, to swap notes and to increase your knowledge.

If you are of a competitive nature then riding must have strong appeal in all fields, especially dressage, show-jumping and horse trials. Throughout the world there are competitions for all ages and all types of horses and ponies.

Throughout all this you must never forget the responsibility that you have to the pony. He is dependent upon you. He may give his all and try his best for you and all he asks in return is a warm bed, to be well groomed and well fed.

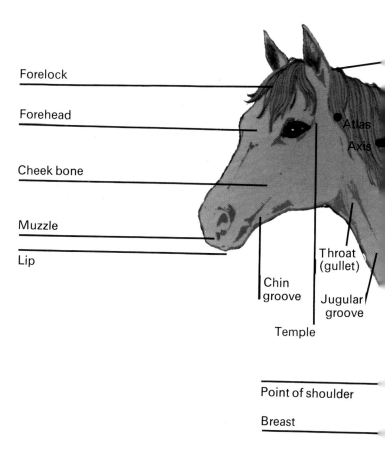

Measure height from ground to withers.

THE POINTS OF A PONY

One of the first things to learn about a pony is his points – terms given to his various physical parts. To be able to understand 'horse' conversation and the 'horsey' language in books, it is essential to know exactly where these various parts are and what they are called. If you hope to work for efficiency tests or examinations you will find that you are asked questions in the early tests on the position of these points.

AGE AND HEIGHT

The age of a horse is established by looking at his teeth. From birth until the age of eight years, it is fairly easy to tell the exact age of a pony. After that age, it becomes much more difficult, and it is impossible therefore to be quite so exact. By studying diagrams and looking at the front teeth or incisors of different ponies it is, with practice, fairly easy to tell. This practice is best obtained with the aid of an experienced person, checking the diagrams against the teeth of ponies whose age is already known. As you become more practised in the art, you can check your progress with each new pony you encounter, comparing your results with the owner's prior knowledge.

All horses and ponies are measured in *hands*. A hand is taken as being 10.16cm (4in). The horse must be standing squarely upon level ground.

Points of a pony

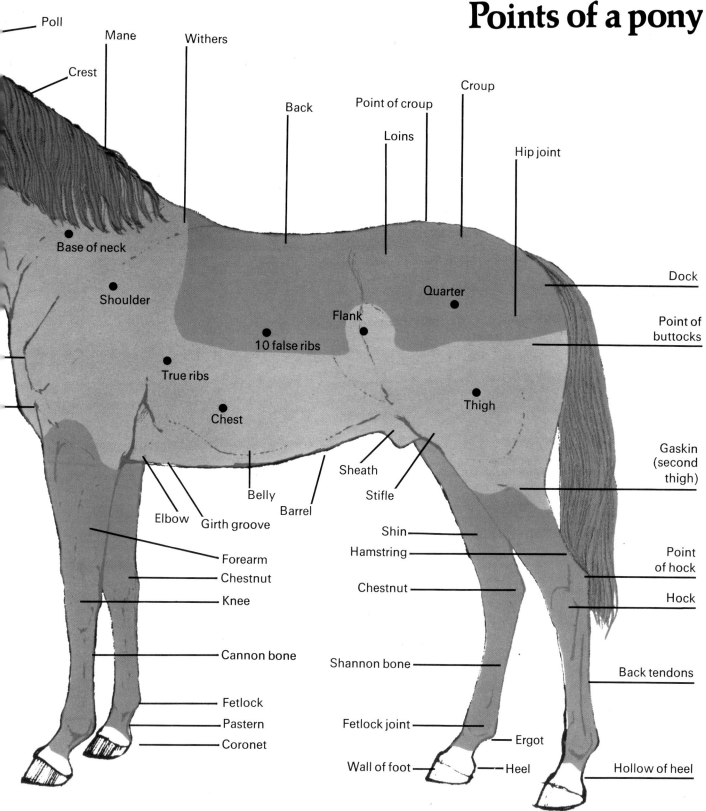

Poll
Mane
Crest
Withers
Back
Point of croup
Croup
Loins
Hip joint
Base of neck
Shoulder
Quarter
Flank
Dock
10 false ribs
True ribs
Chest
Thigh
Point of buttocks
Belly
Sheath
Gaskin (second thigh)
Elbow
Girth groove
Barrel
Stifle
Forearm
Chestnut
Knee
Shin
Hamstring
Chestnut
Point of hock
Hock
Cannon bone
Shannon bone
Back tendons
Fetlock
Pastern
Coronet
Fetlock joint
Ergot
Wall of foot
Heel
Hollow of heel

With a special measuring stick, the exact height is taken from the ground to the withers. Horses are described as ponies up to 14.2 hands and as horses from over 14.2 hands. One of the largest horses on record stood at 18 hands.

CONFORMATION
The shape and build of a pony is called his *conformation*. When looking at a pony first impressions are very important. The type of pony required for learning to ride must be narrow,

well-mannered and a safe ride to give you confidence. Although the pony must seem attractive to you and have a pleasant outlook, it is not necessary for him to be a show pony. Indeed, generally speaking, this type of quality pony is a little too impulsive and bright for the learner.

Look first at the physical points, while the pony is standing naturally on all four legs, but not in a posed position. He should then give a balanced picture. A pony which *stands over* (i.e. when seen from the side, his forelegs appear to be back under

Conformation

him) in front will always tend to go on his forehand (be unbalanced, with more weight over his forelegs). A pony which *stands stretched* (i.e. when seen from the side, his forelegs appear concave below the knee) in front will be difficult to ride up together and will be very likely to move badly.

The hind legs should be well shaped with a good second thigh (the part of the hind leg between the stiple and the hock) and well-developed hocks. The pastern must neither be too long nor too short. Long pasterns are a sign of weakness, whereas short ones may indicate rather choppy strides.

When inspecting the legs, it is best to view them from the front, side and behind. There should be no deviation from the vertical line as this will spoil the paces of the pony. The feet are very important. The pasterns and feet of the hind legs should be more upright than those of the fore legs, because the purpose of the hind feet is to propel the pony forward. The actual wall of the hoof should be smooth and gently sloped from the

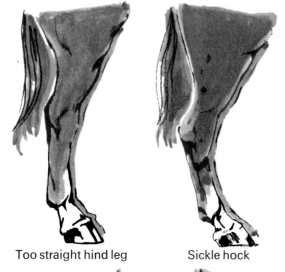

Too straight hind leg   Sickle hock

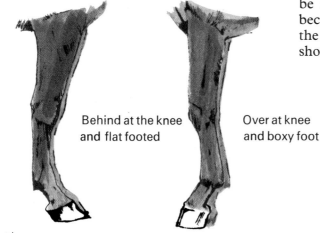

Behind at the knee   Over at knee
and flat footed   and boxy foot

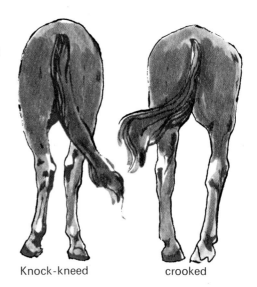

Knock-kneed   crooked

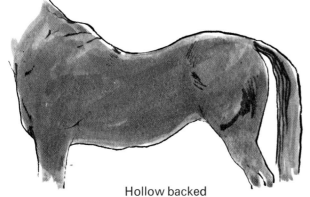

Hollow backed

Straight croup with high set tail

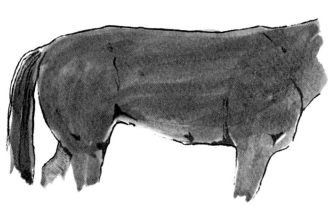

Straight backed

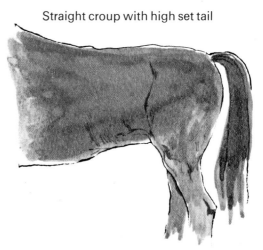

BAD POINTS OF A PONY

coronary band to the ground (see diagram). If there has been any previous history of disease in the foot, this is often indicated by the slope of the foot. There must be no undue roughness. The rest should be well shaped with a large frog.

Boxy feet are upright and narrow, and this is a serious fault. Often ponies with this type of foot have bone ailments within the foot as they age.

The barrel of the pony should be deep, with a good sloping shoulder and withers that are well-defined.

It is preferable for a pony to have good hindquarters that are well-developed and of a reasonable length. If the hindquarters are very short, as in the cob, it is difficult to establish a good swinging stride at a gallop.

The topline, that is the line from the poll along the neck and back, is very important. This topline should rise towards the withers. A pony whose quarters are higher and more developed than the forehand will always give an unbalanced ride. From birth until the age of five years the pony is growing, and most ponies grow each year alter-nately in the hindquarters and forehand. It is therefore quite usual to see a three-year-old with quarters higher and more developed than its forehand. This is why the pony should not be asked to work until he is five. Ponies over the age of five should, if their conformation is good, appear well-balanced. The complete picture of a pony with good conformation and health should be one of alertness and balance, with well set head and neck, making a truly pleasant picture.

When looking at a pony for conformation, it must be remembered that the ideal has been described here. It is essential for a pony to be healthy, sound and capable of doing the work that is required of him. Remember, however, that the perfect pony is still to be born. Although it is hoped that a pony will have many good points of conformation, it is far more important that he is honest, with a kind temperament, pleasant to ride and safe for the beginner. Many show ponies with superb conformation are quite unsuitable for hacking, jumping and the general activities in which you might wish to take part.

A healthy, well-conformed pony.

Saddles

Before you begin to ride you should know something about the equipment you will be using. All leather work – bits, saddles and bridles – is called *tack*. The saddlery is stored in the tack room, near the stable yard. It should be clean, light and warm, with plenty of storage space for saddles, bridles and rugs.

There are three main types of saddle in common use. The first is a general purpose saddle, very good for beginners as it is not exaggerated in design and is perfectly suitable for all forms of riding. The next is the jumping saddle, more elaborate in its design since it is forward cut with a place for the rider's knee when in a jumping seat. The dressage saddle is very straight cut with a deep seat encouraging the rider to sit with a long leather, allowing maximum use of the legs. It has a short Lonsdale girth which fastens low down so that the buckles are not felt through the saddle when the rider has a deep leg position. It is important that the saddle fits not only the rider but also the pony. It is best to have a saddler bring several saddles to the pony to fit the best type for the rider's purpose and the pony's comfort.

Saddles must be cleaned every day to keep them supple and in good condition, and the stitching of all leatherwork checked for wear and

Types of saddles

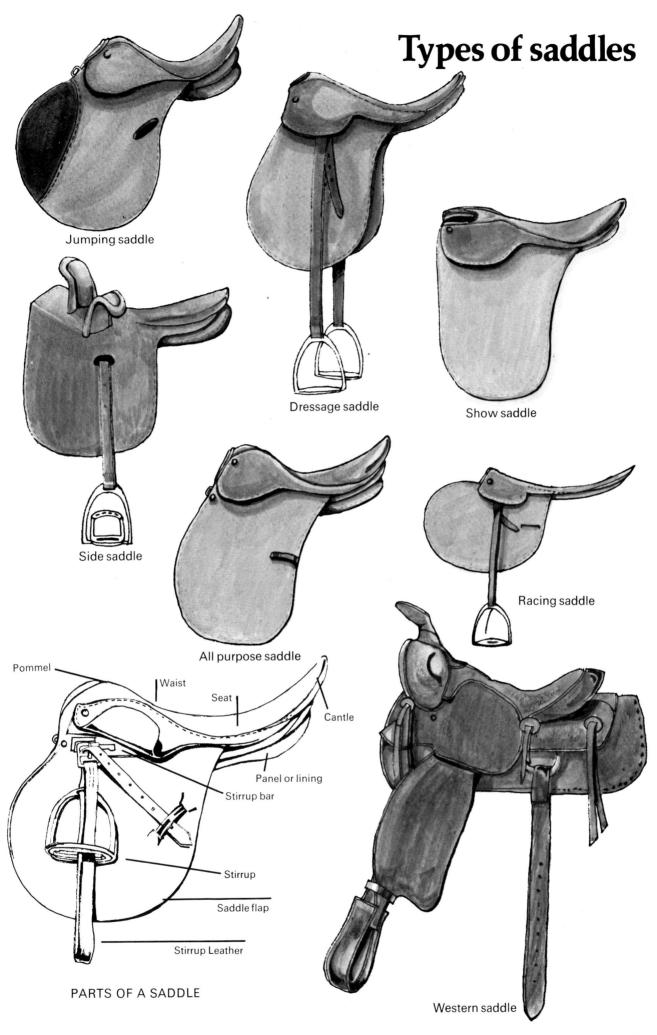

Jumping saddle

Dressage saddle

Show saddle

Side saddle

All purpose saddle

Racing saddle

PARTS OF A SADDLE

Pommel

Waist

Seat

Cantle

Panel or lining

Stirrup bar

Stirrup

Saddle flap

Stirrup Leather

Western saddle

Types of girths

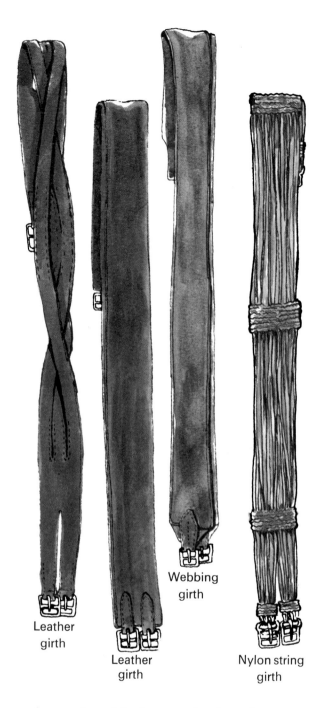

Leather
girth

Leather
girth

Webbing
girth

Nylon string
girth

Saddle cleaning is an important everyday routine

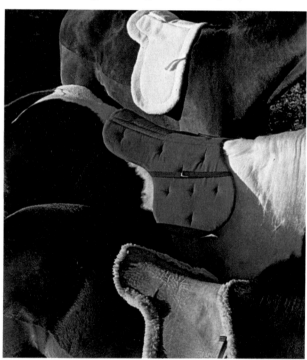

Numnahs should be kept scrupulously clean.

weakness. A saddle horse, a bucket of water, a cloth to clean the leatherwork, a chamois leather to dry it, a soap sponge, saddle soap and a dry cloth for buckles, stirrup irons and bits will be needed. Place the saddle on the saddle horse and remove the leathers. With the wet cloth wash the saddle, leathers and stirrups, being particularly careful to remove grease spots and mud. Dry the leatherwork with a chamois. Finally, with a damp sponge and saddle soap, go over the whole saddle.

Numnahs

These are soft cloths, very often padded or made of sheepskin, which fit underneath the saddle. They are particularly useful on a pony that has a cold back – one that cringes from the feel of leather on his back. For dressage, when the pony has to exert himself in collected work, they ensure that the saddle continues to fit properly. In show jumping, a pony has to use his back to make a big jump, giving it a round outline, and a numnah ensures his comfort throughout. The numnah may be used *as a temporary measure* for a badly fitting saddle. The saddle should fit without a numnah. Numnahs of man-made fibre such as nylon are easy to care for and will usually wash in a washing machine. The sheepskin ones are comfortable for the pony to wear, but require considerably more care to keep clean. They may not fit into a washing machine.

Stirrups

The stirrup, though called an iron, should always be made of stainless steel, as other metals tend to be too soft and will easily break. The iron must be the correct size for the rider's foot. A very small one may cause the foot to become stuck, and a large one may allow the foot to slip through until the ankle is resting on the iron, making it impossible to free the foot in a fall. For the iron to fit properly, there should be 1.25cm ($\frac{1}{2}$in) on either side of the foot.

There are many different designs of stirrup. The most common are shown beneath.

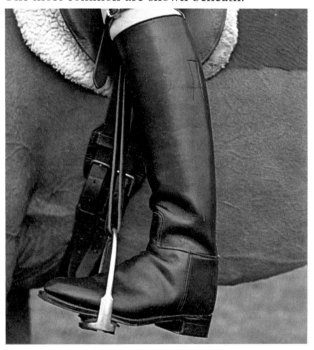

The correct position of the foot.

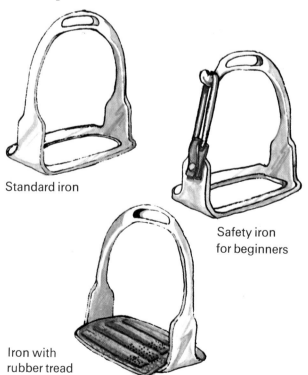

Standard iron

Safety iron
for beginners

Iron with
rubber tread

Bridles and bits

A bridle is used to support the *bit* which lies in the pony's mouth. There are three main types of bridles: the Snaffle, the Pelham and the Double Bridle, the Snaffle being the most common. This is used for normal exercising, when learning to ride, on young ponies and very often for hunting and jumping as well. It is the mildest form of bridle and the one you will use at first.

A properly bridled pony.

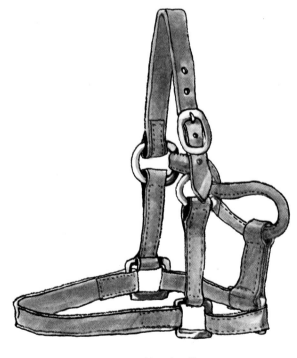

Head collar

Types of bridles

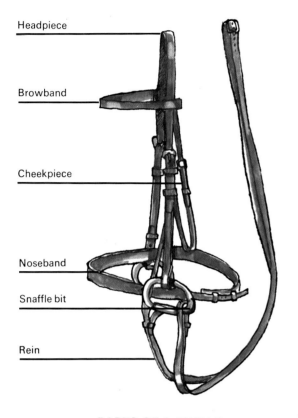

Headpiece

Browband

Cheekpiece

Noseband

Snaffle bit

Rein

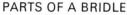

PARTS OF A BRIDLE

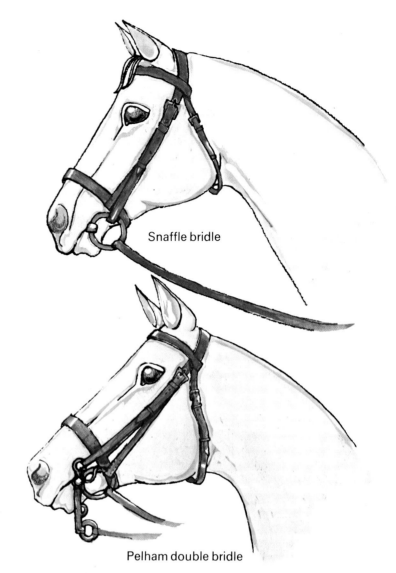

Snaffle bridle

Pelham double bridle

The Snaffle bridle and some Snaffle bits

The first part of a snaffle bridle is the browband which lies in front of the pony's ears. Next is the nose band, which usually lies above the bit below the cheek bones. The head piece goes over the poll and is equally balanced on either side of the pony's head so that the cheek pieces may be attached to it. Next comes the snaffle which is attached to the cheek pieces, and finally the reins which are attached to the bit. The snaffle bit, supported by the bridle, acts on the corners of the mouth and its effect is to raise the pony's head. There are many variations on the snaffle bit: curved, straight bar, jointed or double linked bits made of stainless steel, sometimes covered with rubber or entirely of rubber, perhaps hardened into vulcanite.

The rubber snaffle is a very mild bit made of india rubber with a chain passing through the centre. It is particularly useful for young ponies that are light mouthed and nervous of going to the bit. The eggbut snaffle is a jointed bit with fixed rings which lessens the chances of pinching the lips. It is a popular bit and suits most ponies. The German snaffle is a lightweight bit with a hollow mouthpiece, thick enough to give a widely distributed surface pressure. Most young ponies go kindly in it. The French bridoon, or Gloucester

snaffle, has a double-jointed mouthpiece useful on ponies that are fussy in their mouths. It allows a little more mobility than the normal snaffle and is good for young ponies. The twisted snaffle is a strong bit with loose rings or eggbut rings. The centre piece has a single joint and the actual bit is twisted. It is severe in its action and used only on ponies with very hard mouths. It was more fashionable 30 years ago, though it may still be found in some riding stables today.

The other bits available, such as the pelham, scamperdale, kimblewick and bridoon have more specialized uses – for hacking or jumping – or to overcome problems in specific ponies.

Bitting arrangements

In the correct fitting of a bit in a pony's mouth several factors must be considered: the size of the pony, the shape of his mouth, the work the pony is required to do and the skill of the rider. The snaffle should lie comfortably in the pony's mouth and just wrinkle the corners of the lips. Too wide a bit can cause the front teeth of the pony unnecessary discomfort if the snaffle is jointed, banging the teeth when the action of the rein comes into play. The correct size for the pony is very important. It is also important to clean the bit every day.

Correct way to fit a bridle

1. Slip the reins over the pony's head.

2. Gently open the mouth and slip the bit in.

3. Do up the throat lash.

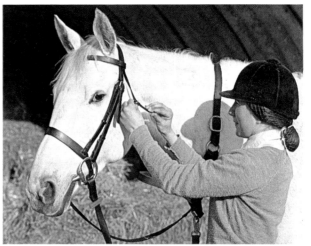

4. Fasten the noseband and check the bridle for fit.

Types of bits

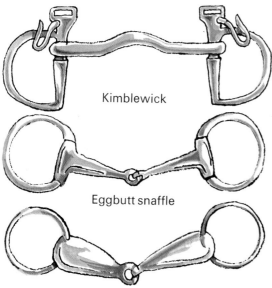

Kimblewick

Eggbutt snaffle

Loose ring German snaffle

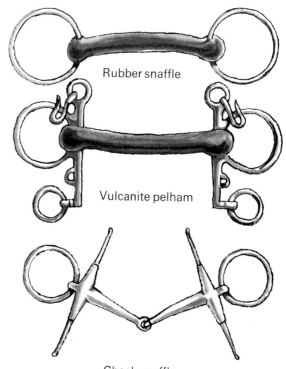

Rubber snaffle

Vulcanite pelham

Cheek snaffle

Grooming

The grooming of the stable pony is very important, not only for appearance, but also for health and good condition. A hoof-pick is used for removing dirt and stones from the sole of the hoof. A dandy brush is fairly stiff and is more often used to remove mud and dirt from the hair of ponies with thick coats living out in fields. The dandy brush must never be used on mane or tail as the stiff bristles would break the hair. The body brush is used for removing scurf and grease from coat, mane and tail. The curry comb is used to clean the body brush, never on the pony. The soft water brush is used to damp the mane and tail to make them lie flat. The mane and tail comb is used for trimming and for thinning the top of the tail. The stable rubber, made of cloth rather like a tea towel, gives a final polish to the groomed pony. The wisp is usually made of hay and is used on fit ponies only to promote circulation and build up muscle. Grooming tools should be kept in a container as they can easily become lost.

Always work from heel to toe with a hoof-pick.

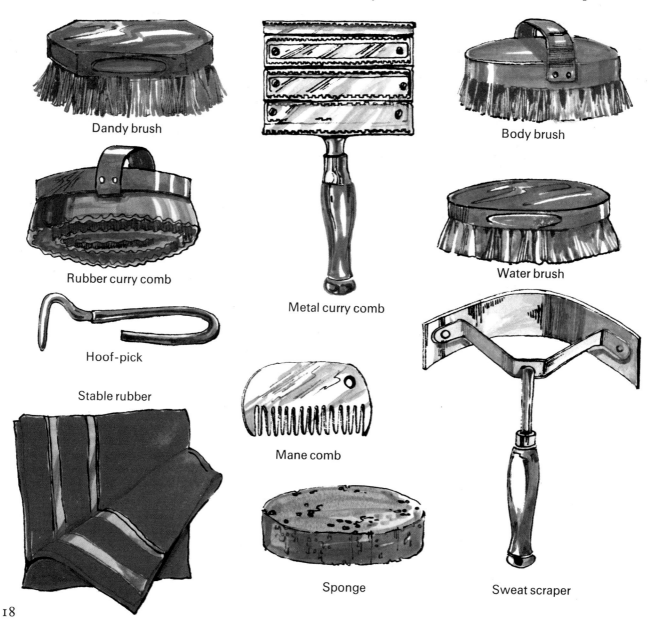

Dandy brush

Metal curry comb

Body brush

Rubber curry comb

Water brush

Hoof-pick

Stable rubber

Mane comb

Sponge

Sweat scraper

Use the body brush with a firm 'to and fro' motion.

Using the mane comb.

The end result – a beautifully groomed pony.

Chapter 2

First lessons

When you start to ride it is important to start correctly. Skill in riding requires knowledge of technique and how to apply it. To be successful you must be patient, sympathetic and learn to understand the pony's mental and physical make up.

I t is essential to take lessons from a qualified instructor at a reputable riding school where the ponies are suitable and safe for teaching beginners. If there is a choice of several riding schools in your area, it is a good idea to take someone with experience to visit them. Look for ponies that are well looked-after, and cheerful, friendly but firm instructors who are well organized. Facilities do not have to be grand, but an enclosed area such as a sand school, where you may ride all year round, is essential. Ask if you are able to hack as lessons progress. This is an excellent way to relax and to enjoy the pony more. You must always have an experienced rider with you when hacking.

Inquire about private lessons. If possible the first few hours of instruction should be private. This allows you to progress at a relaxed rate and

Place the front arch of the saddle in the crook of the elbow when carrying the saddle.

Leather soled shoes or boots are essential.

Mounting

1. Check the girth. Take the reins in the left hand.

Dismounting

1. Remove your feet from the stirrups.

to get to know the pony and the instructor. Early confidence is important. Bad habits develop through nervousness and are extremely difficult to correct later.

Although every precaution may be taken, falls can still happen. It is important, therefore, for you to dress properly. Go to a reputable riding outfitters and buy a hard hat that fits you comfortably and will not fall off, even without a chin strap. Test it with your head between your knees. Jodhpurs are not essential for the first lessons though they do give greater comfort and prevent the soreness that may result from wearing jeans or trousers. Casual shoes that slip on and shoes or sandals with buckles are dangerous. They should never be used for riding. Wellington boots are unsatisfactory as they tend to be too wide and may stick in the stirrup iron. The best footwear is a pair of riding boots. If they are thought too expensive for a beginner then a pair of walking shoes, with laces and leather soles, will do just as well to start.

When you begin to ride, watching more experienced riders will help you. Early lessons should

2. Place your left foot in the iron.

3. Pass the right leg over the pony's back.

2. Spring down from the saddle, holding the front.

3. Land lightly on two feet.

last no longer than half an hour a time, long enough for you to get the feel of riding, yet short enough to avoid overtired muscles or stiffness.

If possible arrange the first twelve lessons in close succession, perhaps three times a week and certainly no less than once a week. This is much better than long lessons with long gaps in between. Ask your instructor if you can help to get the pony ready for a ride. This will help you to get used to grooming, tacking up, and handling the pony. Some instructors give three-quarter-hour lessons to allow time to enable you to help with stabling the pony after the ride. This is good training and you will learn more than if the pony is just brought out and returned for you before and after each of your lessons.

Mounting and dismounting

During your first lesson you may be taught the correct way to mount and dismount. Before you mount make sure that the pony is standing squarely on all four legs. Also check the girth and tighten it if it has been loosened. Take the reins into your left hand. Then place your left foot into the stirrup iron while you face the pony's tail. Grasp the waist of the saddle on the offside with your right hand and lightly spring off your right foot into the saddle as shown in the illustration.

To dismount, first take both feet from the stirrups, hold both reins and stick in your left hand, hold the front of the saddle with your right hand. Swing your right leg behind and over the pony's back and spring lightly to the ground.

Correct seat

A correct seat means the position that you must maintain in the saddle so that you can influence the pony and ride effectively. The seat depends on balance, suppleness and to a lesser degree grip. You must sit square and level in the centre of the saddle.

When you look at someone with the correct seat from the side try to imagine two straight lines, one from the ear of the rider through the shoulders, hip and heels and the other from the elbow through the rider's hand and rein to the bit.

The stirrup leather must be long enough to allow you to rest your foot on the tread of the stirrup and still keep your knee bent, without stiffness. Here is an easy guide to judge the correct length of leather. You should stand to one side of the pony and place the knuckles of the fist of one hand on the stirrup buckle of the saddle and measure the leather and iron from under your armpit along the length of your arm. This gives you a guide to the correct length of leather.

As you become more experienced you will find it easier to adjust your leathers to the required length when mounted.

The correct way to hold the reins

The reins are usually held in both hands in the United Kingdom. When you are sitting on the pony the position of the centre buckle of the reins is at the withers. Place your left hand on top of the left rein and your right hand on top of the right rein. Close your fingers around the rein and allow the reins to come between your little finger and ring finger. It is also correct to have your thumb on top of the rein. The spare loop should fall on the right side of the pony.

If you are learning to ride in the United States you may be taught to hold the reins in one hand. This is part of the direction style of riding.

Sit in the centre of the saddle to achieve a correct seat.

The aids

The aids are the means of communication between you, the rider and the pony. With an aid you can hold a conversation with the pony, speaking gently, firmly, actively, and always positively. The degree of the aid used will depend on the stage of training of the pony and also its temperament and its sensitivity. Some lazy ponies require a fairly strong aid, while other more sensitive ponies will need the lightest possible aid.

The aids may be natural and artificial.

THE NATURAL AIDS

The voice, hands, legs and weight of the body are the natural aids. Each has a purpose on its own and they are sometimes used together.

The voice

Naturally enough, your voice is one means of communication. Ponies are greatly influenced by the human voice. The voice is used in training, when working a horse on the lunge. You can use a quiet calm voice to soothe and encourage the pony and a harsh or sharp voice to reprimand the pony.

Hands

The prime function of the hands is to guide and control the pony. You must develop a sympathetic feeling through the reins, handling them with tact, feeling, and firmness when necessary. The outside rein (the one nearest the fence) regulates the pace and maintains control while the inside rein (the one nearest the centre) gives the bend. Your hand must be completely independent of the rest of your body so that it is free from all involuntary movement. When your hand is used it should be used as lightly as possible. Your fingers squeeze the rein and your arm is drawn back maintaining a straight line from the bit through the rein to your hand and elbow.

The legs

Your legs create the impulsion or energy which moves the pony forward and also controls the quarters. The inside leg controls and maintains the impulsion, while the outside leg controls the quarters.

The weight of the body

Your head, shoulders, back and seat all make the complete weight of the body. The weight must go down through a straight back and into your seat for the weight to be of value and effect with slowing down aids. You must try to sit still. In this way you will be closer to your pony and a greater benefit and effect will be achieved by the body weight. Sitting crookedly will unbalance the pony.

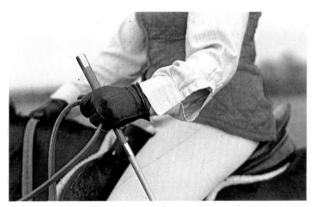

The correct way to grip the reins.

Hands guide the horse and should be used lightly.

Whips are used to reinforce the aids from the leg.

Types of whips

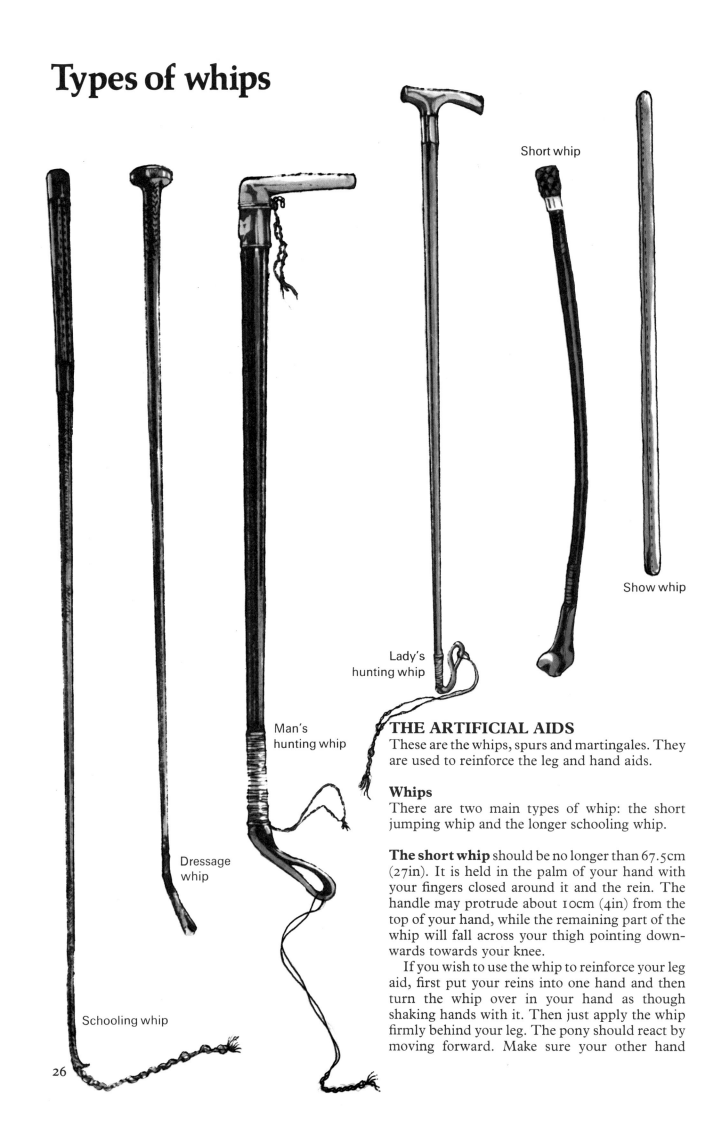

Short whip

Show whip

Lady's hunting whip

Man's hunting whip

Dressage whip

Schooling whip

THE ARTIFICIAL AIDS

These are the whips, spurs and martingales. They are used to reinforce the leg and hand aids.

Whips

There are two main types of whip: the short jumping whip and the longer schooling whip.

The short whip should be no longer than 67.5cm (27in). It is held in the palm of your hand with your fingers closed around it and the rein. The handle may protrude about 10cm (4in) from the top of your hand, while the remaining part of the whip will fall across your thigh pointing downwards towards your knee.

If you wish to use the whip to reinforce your leg aid, first put your reins into one hand and then turn the whip over in your hand as though shaking hands with it. Then just apply the whip firmly behind your leg. The pony should react by moving forward. Make sure your other hand

Types of martingales

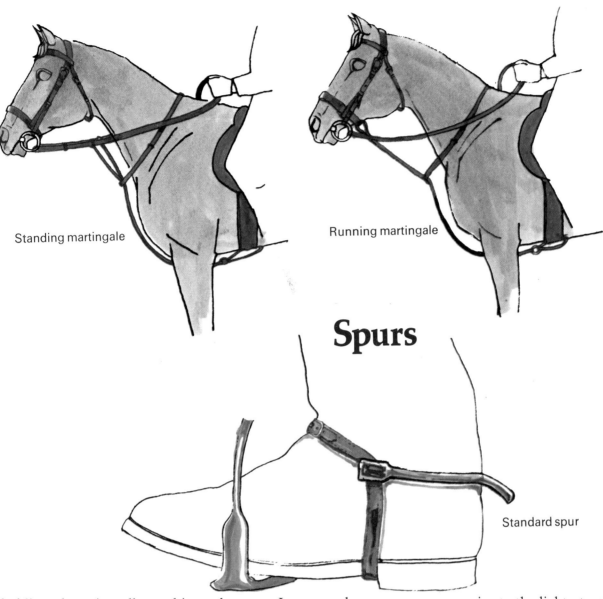

Standing martingale

Running martingale

Spurs

Standard spur

holding the reins allows this to happen. Immediately replace the whip to the normal position and re-take the reins into both hands.

The schooling whip is considerably longer than the jumping whip and may not be used competitively. As the name suggest it is really designed for training the pony to respond to the aids well. It is carried in the same way as the jumping whip. However, because it is usually about a metre long it comes over your thigh and with a flick of the wrist you can reinforce the leg aid without taking your hand off the rein. The schooling whip is more difficult to handle and should be used only by experienced riders. The beginner's hands may be unsteady and cause the whip to come into play unnecessarily.

Spurs

These should only be used by riders with considerable experience. Their purpose is to make the pony very responsive to the lightest possible aid and should not be worn by learners and inexperienced riders.

Martingales

There are two main types of martingale: the running and the standing. Both are used to prevent the pony from putting his head too high and therefore beyond an angle of control.

The standing martingale is attached from the girth between the pony's forelegs to a cavesson noseband. It should be at such a length that it is effective only if the pony puts his head too high.

The running martingale is attached at one end between the pony's forelegs to the girth. At the other end it is divided into two straps with a ring on the end of each strap. These rings pass around the reins. Again the martingale will only come into effect if the pony raises his head beyond an angle of control. It is useful when jumping.

Application of the aids

The pony will first be introduced to the simple aids in the stable. When strapping or mucking out the groom will need to move the pony from one side of the box to the other. The simplest way to do this is to say 'over' while gently pressing your hand against the pony's side. The pony will associate the feeling and the voice and will gradually learn what the word means and move over. As soon as the pony shows that he understands he must be praised with an encouraging word or a titbit.

When training the pony to understand the aids you are developing the pony's response to voice, weight and touch. Before you are able to train a pony to understand the aids, you must develop a secure and well-balanced seat so that the coordination of your leg and hand can be used independently of one another. In sports such as athletics, tennis, gymnastics and dancing you use your hands and arms to balance the rest of your body. In riding it is not possible. If your hands and arms moved in an involuntary fashion the aids would most certainly confuse the pony. So, when learning to ride you must establish a good, firm and independent seat first.

To halt
Sit still in the saddle with a straight back. Close both legs to the pony's sides and quietly pull on the reins. As soon as the pony halts relax your hand and allow him to stand still for a few moments.

Walk on
To make the pony walk on, sit straight in the saddle, vibrate or tap both legs at the girth and ease the contact on the reins to allow the pony to walk forward. As the pony walks on try to maintain a steady, light contact throughout. At all times you should be sitting up, looking ahead, with your arms relaxed falling straight to the elbows, with your elbows bent to make a straight

line from them through your hand to the pony's mouth. Your knee should be bent with your lower leg close to the pony's barrel and your heels down. To make the pony walk actively your legs should be applied alternately left and right. The pony's head will bob up and down.

The right turn
Here the aids are diagonal. This means that your right leg will be on the girth and your left leg behind the girth. The pony will be bent to the right, the left rein being the balance or support rein just allowing the bend. In making any turn either left or right it is important to give the pony time to understand the signal. All ponies are greatly affected by the rider's weight so to make a smooth turn to either direction first look to the direction that you wish to travel. In that way your weight is in the direction you want to turn. Keep your shoulders parallel to the pony's. This will make it easier for the pony to maintain his balance and to obey the request.

A perfect right turn

1. **Bend the pony to the right.**

2. **Keep the right leg on the girth and the left behind.**

3. **Your shoulder should be parallel to the pony's.**

4. **Maintain your weight in the right direction.**

Trot

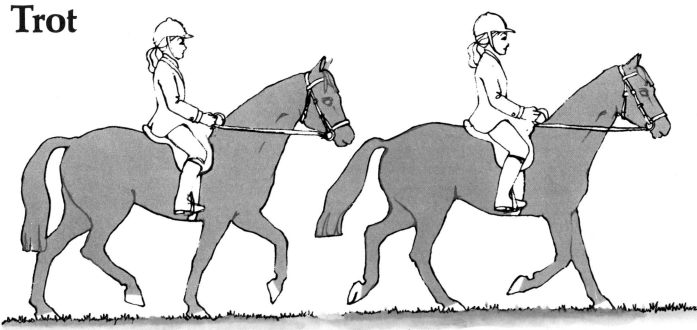

During the trot, the pony's legs move in diagonal pairs as can be seen here.

Canter

The canter is a pace of three times and is perhaps the most comfortable pace for pony and rider.

The rising trot

The trot is a pace of two-time, which means that the pony's legs move in diagonal pairs. The left diagonal pair is the off fore and the near hind. When riding at the trot you must sit on one diagonal and rise on the other. At first you may have difficulty in keeping your balance and rising to the trot. It is important to keep your hands still to avoid injuring the pony's mouth. When you first begin the rising trot, you may have to hold onto the pony's mane to prevent him from being injured. While in rising trot your lower leg should be still with your knee bent and heel down. Your leg should remain close to the girth. It is helpful to watch a good rider first so that you have a picture in your mind of what actually happens. Try not to rise too high to start with and allow the pony to do the work by tossing you up and down.

The sitting trot

For the sitting trot you should maintain the same attitude in the saddle as you had at walk and halt. Sit centrally in the saddle, in the lowest part of it with shoulders falling above your hips and your hips above your heels.

The sitting trot is used in all changes of pace; that is from walk to trot, trot to canter, canter to trot, trot to walk. It is more tiring for both you and the pony and should not be used on very young ponies. As you and the pony become more experienced, the sitting trot is used to enable you to achieve more advanced movements.

The aids to trot

At this stage all changes of pace will be progressive. This means that if you wish to increase the pace from halt the procedure will be halt,

walk, trot. The aid for trot therefore will be from a walk. Sit still and straight in the saddle, maintain contact with the pony's mouth and close both legs firmly to urge the pony into trot. The first few steps are best taken at sitting trot, as you can apply and carry out the aids most effectively.

The canter

The canter is a pace of three time. This means the legs move in three definite beats. The series of the legs on the left rein left canter would be off-hind, right diagonal i.e. off-fore and near hind together and finally the near fore leg. This last leg to leave the ground is called the leading leg.

In canter, sit tall, straight and squarely in the saddle just as you do at the halt, walk and sitting trot. You will find that canter is a very comfortable pace. The pony will bob his head up and

down and you should allow this to happen by maintaining a light contact on the pony's mouth.

The aids to canter

First establish a sitting trot and maintain a correct position in the saddle. Then position the pony in the direction that you wish to travel by bending the pony to that direction with the inside rein, placing your inside leg on the girth, keeping your outside leg behind the girth. The outside rein keeps the balance or support. Apply both legs firmly and the pony still strike off into the canter in the direction of the bend. To clarify the aid for canter right:

Right bend.
Right leg on the girth.
Left leg behind the girth.
Left rein to balance and support the right.

Use of hands

1. **The correct position of the hands and reins.**

2. **The wrong way to try to control the pony.**

3. **The hands resist to slow the pony's pace.**

4. **Give the pony its head when approaching a jump.**

More about hands

The hands three functions: they act, they resist and they give. The hands, through the pony's reins and the bit control, receive the power, impulsion and energy that is created by the rider's legs. The hands also guide and control the shoulders, neck and head of the pony. Looking at each statement in turn it is easy to see how important it is to develop good hands.

They act. The hand will act, whenever it has a definite movement to direct, for example in the right turn, the hand acts by leading the pony by feeling strongly on the right rein.

They resist. The hand resists when the speed of the horse slows down. It may resist slightly when regulating the energy coming from the pony's hindquarters.

They give. This is very important whenever the pony has responded well to your instructions. The hand will lighten and allow the pony forward. After schooling or working the pony quite hard the hand will give to allow the pony to walk on a long rein stretching his head and neck in a relaxed manner. As you become more advanced and start jumping, the hand will give to allow the pony freedom of head and neck over the fence.

The manège

This is the area where both you and the pony may be given your first lessons. An indoor school is ideal because it provides a place to ride without distractions and in all weathers.

A manège may be made simply by using a corner of a field, preferably with a hedge or wall down one side and with the other three sides marked by cones, barrels or apple boxes. For your first lessons, however, it is best to have an enclosed area, fenced on all four sides. Many riding schools have a manège with an all-weather surface, possibly sand, enclosed with a post and rail fence. It is helpful for it to be the correct novice dressage arena size of 20 metres by 40 metres (22yd by 44yd). The sides should be marked with large capital letters in the sequence: A, K, E, H, C, M, B, F. These letters can be

remembered by the sentence: All King Edward's Horses Call Me Beautiful Fool.

The manège should always be rectangular in shape, in order to ride turns, circles and straight lines. This combination of movements gives variety to the pony's work and gives you the opportunity to practise and improve coordination of the aids. When riding in the manège, the inside rein is considered to be the rein that is nearer the centre of the manège, the outside rein the one nearer the wall or fence. In all school movements, the rider must remember to look to the direction of travel.

Turning. You must remember first to look in the direction of the turn and then to apply the aids. The pony is led in the direction you wish to go with the inside rein, while your inside leg maintains the impulsion. The outside rein goes towards the inside rein as a support, but must not

Riding a circle

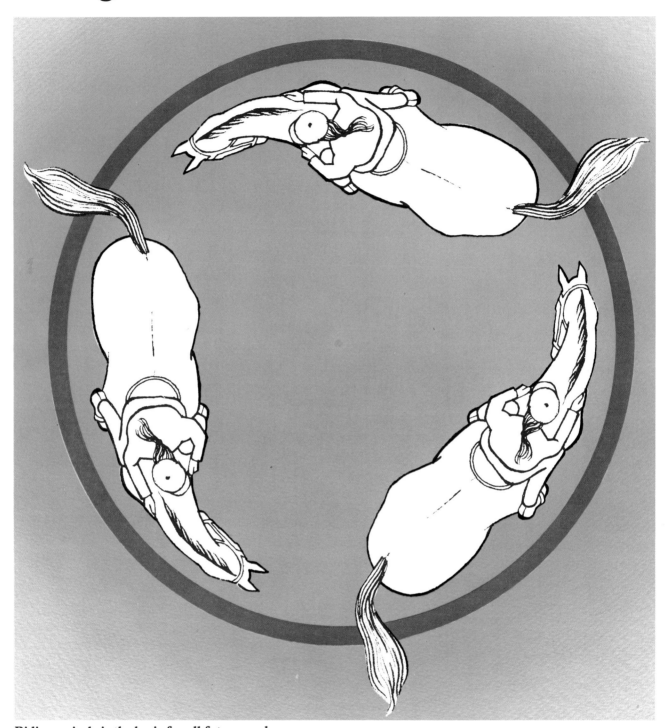

Riding a circle is the basis for all future work.

cross to the other side of the pony's neck. Your outside leg helps to control the hindquarters.

The Americans train their horses slightly differently. Because the rider holds the reins in one hand, the horse learns to respond to the touch of the reins on the neck, and turns in the direction of the touch. This is known as neck-railing.

Riding a circle. It is important to learn to ride a circle well, as it is the basis for all future work. The pony is first positioned in the direction of the circle, bent the way he will be going. Your inside leg is placed at the girth to control the hindquar-

ters. The outside rein allows the bend in the inside and regulates the pace.

First circles should be the maximum diameter of 20m (22yd) touching the track on each long side of the arena. As you become more proficient, smaller circles may be practised, 15m (16yd), 12m (13yd) and 10m (11yd) diameter.

Riding a straight line is a difficult exercise for both you and the pony. Aids must be so well controlled that the pony is not tempted to swing his quarters to left or right. The footfall of the left hind leg should follow the same track as the left fore leg and the same with right feet. It is most

Figure of eight

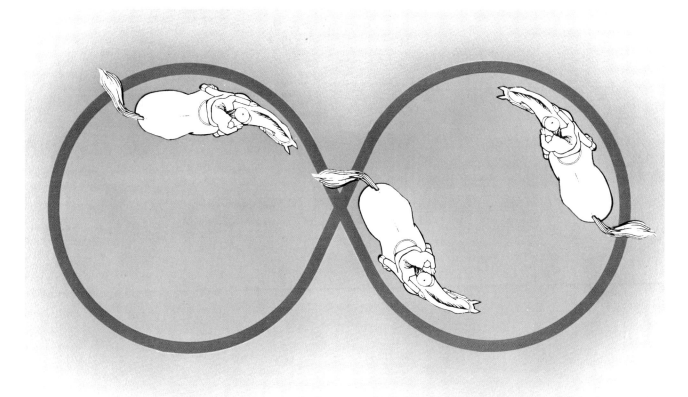

The figure of eight needs to be ridden on an obedient and supple pony.

important for you to sit in the centre and lowest part of the saddle, looking straight ahead, with your hips and shoulders parallel to those of the pony. An even contact on each rein must be maintained and both your legs firmly applied to the barrel of the pony.

As soon as the first schooling lessons, with simple turns and circles, have been mastered it is time to work on more complicated exercises. The manège and the exact position of its markers become more familiar, as do the following basic terms applied to them.

The track is the outer edge of the arena just inside the markers and is the usual track that the pony will take. Sometimes inside and outside tracks are referred to. The outside track is the original course just inside the markers, and the inside track is a line about 1.5m (5ft) inside them.

Go large is the command given when a movement has been completed and the instructor wishes you to return to the outside track.

Leading file is the rider in the front, usually one of the more experienced riders in the class, who regulates the pace.

Rear file refers to the person at the back of the ride, usually a more experienced rider.

Right rein and **left rein.** You are on the right rein when you and the pony are going round the manège in a clockwise direction with your right hand nearest the centre of the arena. Left rein is movement in an anti-clockwise direction with your left hand nearest the centre of the manège.

Change of rein is when the direction is changed from one rein, either left or right, to the opposite one. There are many ways of doing this, by turns, circles, inclines and serpentines.

Serpentines are loops, either shallow curves or deep half circles. They are excellent exercises for improving the suppleness and balance of the pony. Also, they keep you prepared and make you apply aids well.

Serpentines may be varied by making more loops, possibly four or five. They may be large or small, from track to track or along the centre line.

Figure of eight is an exercise that may be ridden at the walk, trot or canter. At the canter it is necessary to make a transition to trot and walk on the centre line in the centre of the figure, changing the canter lead. The exercise is then called *simple change of lead*. It is best to learn the figure of eight at the walk, first learning to make the correct shape. The simple change of lead should not be tried until you and the pony are able to canter effortlessly on either lead. The shape for the figure of eight in a novice arena is inclined by riding two inclines across the school. The in-

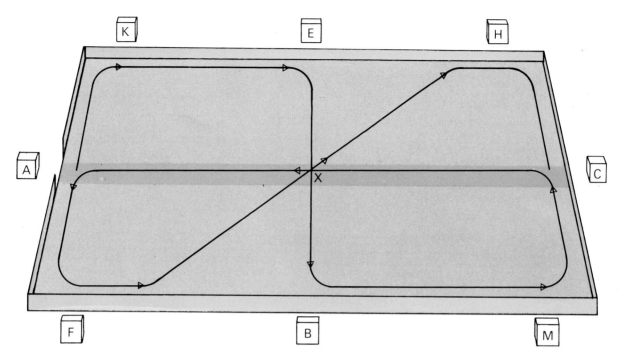

The course for riding a serpentine.

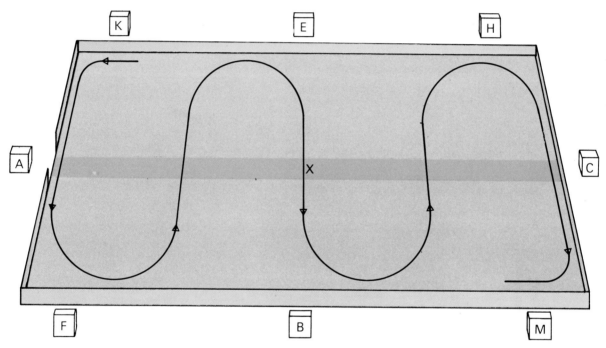

The course for riding an incline.

structor will ask for the movement to commence at A or C. For example if the command is 'At C, begin a large figure of eight', you are on the left rein. At C, the bend to the left is established and at H, left incline to F. Then on the right rein the right incline from K is completed at M.

Inclines are a convenient way of changing the rein by inclining diagonally across the manège either from a quarter marker to the opposite quarter marker or from a quarter to the half marker. Another way to incline is from the centre line to the outside track. When riding inclines the aids are applied diagonally with the inside leg on the girth and the outside leg behind. The pony's direction is made with the inside rein and as with all school movements, it is important for you to look in the direction of travel.

Musical rides
These are tremendous fun once you are proficient in simple school movements. A series of school movements are linked together to make patterns. The music helps you to relax and develop a better feel for rhythm and pace. Musical rides require precision, quick reactions and teamwork. These disciplines encourage improvement in balance and coordination of aids.

Riding without reins helps the rider achieve good balance.

Working without stirrups

In all school work and early lessons you must strive to develop a deep and independent seat. Working without stirrups is a good way to improve the depth, balance and suppleness of the seat. This helps to make you relax your hips, loins and thighs, allowing your legs to come longer down the saddle and deepening the thigh. The deeper and better balanced the seat becomes, the easier it is to apply the aids well with good coordination and maximum results. In the exercises to improve the seat, take care not to work too long without stirrups. In the first lessons, two or three minutes are ample, but this time can be lengthened as confidence increases. In the early stages of training, 20 minutes is the maximum time you should work without stirrups. Musical rides without stirrups are excellent to improve balance, coordination and depth of seat in an amusing and challenging manner. Never begin a lesson without stirrups. Wait until the pony has had the opportunity to limber up and relax his back, usually about ten minutes into a lesson.

Working on the lunge.

Working on the lunge

A few of the exercises that can be done on the lunge to improve balance and correct attitude in the saddle.

Lunge lessons

Working on the lunge is the best way to develop a deep seat. Lunge work improves balance and correct attitude in the saddle, while developing a feel for the pony through all movements. On the lunge, you can concentrate on your own faults and then learn to correct them without having to worry about controlling the pony which should be obedient and well-balanced. The instructor controls the pony on a long line while you, on the pony, make large circles around the instructor.

To begin with you will find that 20 minutes on the lunge is quite enough. You should not work too energetically until you are sufficiently fit. Ideally, 20 minutes every day on the lunge is the best way to establish a well-balanced seat. If this is not possible, then once or twice a week is still helpful and allows you to improve at a slower pace. Simple exercises on the lunge will improve suppleness and athletic ability, build up good coordination and establish a good seat.

At the halt the instructor should place you in a correct position in the saddle. You must be able to maintain this correct attitude, at halt and walk before beginning work at the trot. Nearly all work on the lunge is done without stirrups. Work at the trot should not begin until you are confident in the walk. Hold onto the front of the saddle lightly with two hands. This establishes confidence. Gradually, as you become better balanced and closer to the pony, try holding on with one hand, and then just one finger, until balance and confidence are such that the movement of the pony can be followed without holding.

There are many exercises on the lunge to help you become more relaxed, better balanced and coordinated. It is important that these exercises are carried out well, without loss of good position. They should not be so strenuous that you are struggling to maintain your balance. If at any time throughout a lunge lesson you feel your position is lost, then both hands should be returned to the front of the saddle so that the seat is properly corrected.

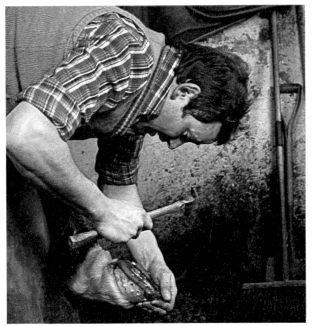

The farrier at work

A day at the farrier

A farrier must pay particular attention to a pony's feet, as the horn of the hoof is growing all the time. If the pony works a lot on the roads, he will need new shoes frequently; working on soft ground, bridle paths, fields or even on indoor school, he will require to be reshod only occasionally or may not need shoes at all. Every month or six weeks, whether the pony needs new shoes or not, the farrier should take off the shoes and trim the feet. The same shoes can be replaced, if they are not worn, though using new nails. This process is called a *refit*.

If the pony is working quite hard, he may need shoeing as often as every three weeks, or he may have pulled off a shoe in deep going, requiring an earlier farrier's visit than usual. There are many signs that a pony may be due for re-shoeing. A loose shoe is easy to recognize when the feet are picked out during grooming. It will also be heard on road exercise. A thin shoe can be due to overall wear, so the pony has difficulty in maintaining a good grip, or it may be thin in a particular area such as the toe, heel, or quarters. A risen clench is a loose and raised nail. Casting a shoe means the actual loss of a shoe. An overgrown foot is when it has become too long through rapid growth and has lost its good shape.

To understand the actual shoeing process, which requires great skill from the farrier, it is necessary to have a basic knowledge of the structure of the pony's foot. The wall of the foot is a very strong, horny substance and grows downwards from the coronet. The sole is the underside of the hoof and protects this part of the foot. The frog can be clearly seen at the heel of the sole. It is nature's anti-slip device, being strong and like rubber. It also prevents the leg from receiving too much of a jar against hard ground. The outer wall of the hoof is strong and insensitive. The inner wall is divided from it by the white line. The farrier must never allow his nails to penetrate this white line. Watching the farrier at work, it is easy to see how skilled he must be and how careful if he is not to injure the pony's foot.

PARTS OF THE HOOF

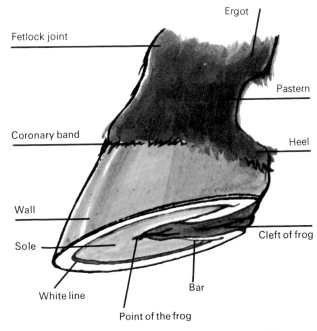

Fetlock joint

Ergot

Pastern

Coronary band

Heel

Wall

Sole

Cleft of frog

White line

Bar

Point of the frog

Chapter 3

Riding away from school

Riding away from the security of the enclosed manège or school is essential for your advancement, but you should not start hacking until you are confident in all paces in the enclosed area.

T he pony must be safe, obedient and as reliable in traffic as in open spaces. The pony is usually more interested and energetic when hacking, and you are able to relax, enjoy the countryside and improve your riding technique without formal tuition. Large open spaces and uneven terrain are ideal for you to develop natural balance and security, first by walking and trotting up and down hills and finally by working at the canter.

Ponies are naturally greedy and may dive at grass and hedgerows, pulling the reins out of your hands. Small ponies can be fitted with grass reins which are attached from the bit to the head piece and then to the D's of the saddle. These reins should not be fitted tightly, but just long enough to prevent the pony from putting his head down and reaching the grass. Ponies should not be allowed to eat when they are out. Grass verges

41

and hedgerows may contain dangerous rubbish or poisonous plants (see page 42) or have been sprayed recently with harmful chemicals. Excessive feeding while exercising can cause colic.

A pony may buck if he is uncomfortable, if the saddle fits badly or presses down too heavily and gives him a sore back, or if you are too heavy for him. If this does happen try to keep his head up and prevent him from putting it between his knees. If he is ridden firmly forward in this way, he will have less chance of unseating you.

Some ponies are nervous of unusual objects sometimes found by hedgerows, such as paper bags, tins or road signs. Reassure him by telling him that all is well and ride him firmly forward with both legs.

As a beginner you should go hacking with an experienced person. Pupil's pony and instructor's horse should both be absolutely reliable. Confidence can be lost very easily after a bad experience. It would be a great mistake to ride out on a friend's pony on your first hack, even if the friend comes with you. He will not be as experienced as your instructor, and the pony may be quite unsuitable, giving you a frightening and possibly dangerous ride.

Country code

Riding in the open country is a lovely way to see out-of-the-way places that are too remote to see by car. It is also an excellent way to develop natural balance and security thus improving your technique without formal teaching. There are, however, many rules of the countryside that you must observe, which have been established to keep the countryside a pleasant place for those who live there as well as for occasional visitors.

All gates must be closed even when there is no livestock. You may be lucky enough to have a local landowner who will let you ride through the woods, over heathland and fields. But always remember that you are his guest and be courteous and considerate. Avoid cutting up the land on wet going. Keep to all tracks and remember that you are not the only one to use the land.

There are certain tracks where you are entitled to ride. These are usually well-signposted and in some districts they are marked on posts and trees. You are not allowed to build a jump or cut down trees and branches to build one on a bridle way. These paths are to be used by everyone, so it is inconsiderate to block a path with a jump.

Learn about the country code and all you can about your hacking country. Get to know local farmers and the men who work for them. Always smile and ride thoughtfully across the land so that you become accepted as part of the countryside. Always use the *headland*, the term used for the outer edge of the field where the crops do not grow. Try to keep off cultivated land as much as possible especially after heavy rain when the ground is wet.

When passing any livestock keep your pony in walk and ride quietly past. At lambing time be particularly careful not to disturb any sheep and

The first few minutes of the first outside ride are best led by the instructor.

Opening and shutting a gate

1. The lead rider should open the gate......

2. ......move it back......

3. ......allow the others to pass through......

4. ......and shut it for them.

avoid riding too close to them. Milking cattle must never be disturbed. Ride through fields at a walk, keeping well away from the cows. Remember that bulls can be very dangerous so never enter a field where there is a bull.

The countryside is enjoyed by all sorts of people who have just as much right to enjoy it as you and your pony. Be especially careful when you ride past anyone you meet. Ask people with dogs to put them on a lead or hold them close because your pony may be nervous of a dog and could tread on it.

Road safety

Ponies are unpredictable. You must learn how to control them on the roads and how to behave there yourself. It is better not to take a pony onto the busy highway, but this may be unavoidable in some areas if there is to be any riding outside the security of the enclosed school. You must know the Highway Code and obey traffic lights and road

signs. Before taking to the road, you must be competent, able to walk, trot and canter and control the pony with reins in one hand.

Here are some points to consider before riding on the roads:

The pony must be suitable, traffic proof and not nervous.

Saddle, bridle stitching and girth must be checked for safety.

Stirrups must be the correct size for your foot.

The pony must be well shod. Loose, badly worn or badly fitting shoes are dangerous.

At night, wear fluorescent arm bands or jacket and a light attached to the stirrup iron. Better still, avoid riding in the dark.

A well fitting hard hat is essential at all times.

Riding boots or lace up shoes are best, as they can be easily released from the stirrup iron in an emergency.

All riders should insure themselves against claims in case injury should be caused to someone else when out riding.

Always use hand signals when moving towards the centre of the road.

When you are actually on the road:

Keep alert at all times, anticipating possible difficulties such as road works, lorries, etc., avoiding these when possible when planning the route to be taken.

Keep to the left side of the road. Keep the pony under control with equal contact on both reins and legs firmly round the pony.

Make movements clear to other road users and ensure that the road is safe before stopping or turning.

When overtaking an obstacle such as a stationary car, look behind first to make sure the road is clear. Signal the intention to pass with outstretched hand, fingers close together.

At junctions or crossroads, keep the pony on a tight rein to prevent him slipping. Road studs should ideally be fitted, especially when trotting on roads.

Ride firmly and confidently when passing a hazard, such as road works. Speak to the pony to reassure him. Do not look at the obstacle.

Whenever possible ride on grass verges, though never on mown grass in front of private houses. In some counties riding on particular verges may be forbidden. Always check.

Be courteous at all times to other people on the road.

Always thank cars and trucks who may slow down for you by raising the hand nearer the middle of the road.

There must always be an instructor, mounted on a reliable and safe horse, in charge of a group ride to control the traffic, cope with junctions and so on.

Less experienced ponies or riders should be on the inside nearest the verge, with an experienced animal on the outside. The group must keep close together as one body, each pony about 1.2m (4ft) from the rear of the one in front. A group should be no larger than six riders. More than that should be split into several groups with a gap between them and one rider in charge of each group. The gap should allow cars to overtake and pull in between groups.

The instructor in charge should always thank other road users. Be courteous to other people you may meet while out on your ride.

Sometimes it may be necessary to lead a pony on the road, to turn him out in his field or if he goes lame on a ride. If riding one and leading another, ride with the led one on your inside nearer the verge.

When leading a pony on foot, walk on the left side of the road but place yourself between the traffic and the pony, that is on his right.

Always ride and lead a pony with a bridle. It is dangerous to try to control a pony in a head collar or halter on the road.

There are four important hand signals which you must learn before riding on the road. These hand signals tell other people on the road what your exact intentions are. Make sure they are given clearly and in plenty of time.

RIDING AT NIGHT

Riding at night can be hazardous and should be avoided if at all possible. There are bound to be times when it cannot be helped, perhaps hacking home from a horse show or hunting, when it is wise to be prepared. Wear light coloured clothing or better still, fluorescent clothing which is obtainable from shops which sell clothing for cyclists or from your local tack shop. If possible, a lamp should be worn on the chest and back. Stirrup lamps are also available for attaching to the stirrup iron. A person on foot leading a pony at night should wear fluorescent clothing and carry a torch.

COMING HOME

On arrival at the stable in the evening, your pony will be tired and should be bedded down as quickly as possible. His bed should be deep and the straw well shaken. Remove the pony's tack, groom him lightly, removing any sweat and mud and re-rug him. When this is done, make sure that the pony has completely cooled down before he has a small feed and is left in peace to relax. While the pony is eating, you may clean his tack. Finally, return to the pony to check that he has eaten up and that all is safe and well for the evening.

**Fluorescent jackets
should be worn for night riding.**

45

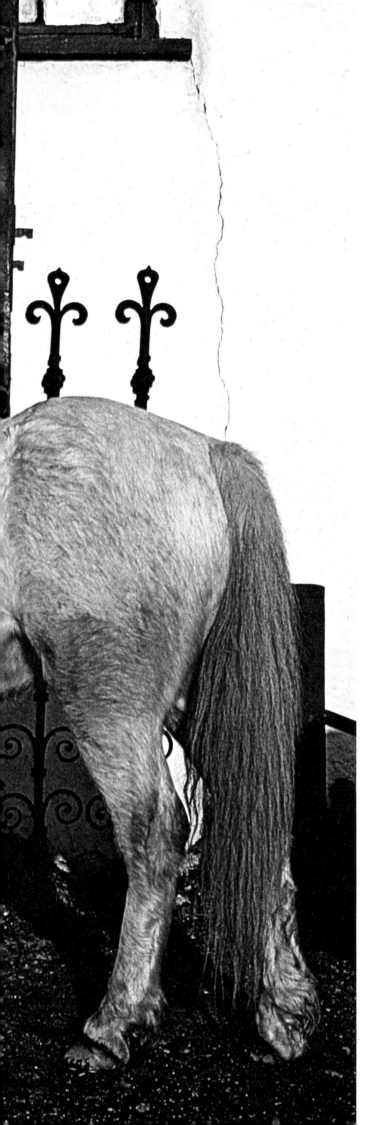

Chapter 4

Keeping a pony

Once you have decided that you enjoy riding and working with ponies, you may wish to own one of your own. This is a very serious undertaking but one that can be very rewarding.

It is very common practice to keep a pony at grass. Most ponies certainly prefer to live out in a field as it gives them more freedom than living in stable.

The pony will need 1.2 to 1.6 hectare (3 to 4 acres) of well-fenced pasture. The type of fencing is of utmost importance for the safety of the pony. If it is too weak the pony may wander onto busy roads and cause a fatal accident. Barbed wire fences may cause injury to the pony as ponies are inquisitive and may well rub against the fence or paw at it with their hooves.

Here are some common types of fencing.
Hedges can make suitable fencing, provided they are thick and are regularly looked at to make sure that there are no holes. The hedge also provides a certain amount of shade in hot weather and is a wind brake and shelter in wet or windy weather.

Keeping
a pony at grass

Post and rail is the best form of fencing as it is really secure, and there can be no risk of injury to the pony. It is extremely long-lasting and needs very little maintenance, though it is very expensive.

Stone walls are another very good and practical form of fencing where stone is readily available.

Plain wire is a fairly inexpensive form of fencing and safe provided that it is always pulled tight. It

is best used in five strands but the danger is that a pony may paw at the lower strands and snap the wire. Although this will not injure the pony, it does of course weaken the fence which will therefore need constant checking. It is not ideal except as a temporary measure.

Top rail and three strands of wire is a compromise type of fencing. The top is composed of post and rail, and the lower part of tight, single strands of wire. This makes it difficult for the pony to weaken the top of the fence by pushing or to force a way through to the other side.

Strip grazing with electric fencing. Strip grazing is resting one part of the land while another part is used for grazing. A simple and effective way of doing this is to use an electric fence. Ponies learn quickly. They will sniff and touch an electric fence and receive a small shock. They will not go near it again. The first time that an electric fence is used, it is important to stay with the pony until he knows what it is, just in case he should be nervous and panic. It is most unusual for ponies to worry about electric fencing, and it is an excellent method of getting the best use from pasture.

Ponies cannot continually live in the same field. They are wasteful grazers and will only eat the grasses they like. Ponies' droppings cause continuously grazed pasture to become sourso they must be removed in order to preserve the pasture. The field must be rested, rolled, harrowed and limed or fertilized. The grass first begins to grow in April, May and June and during these months it is advisable to rest some pasture so that the pony is not able to graze over a large area, soiling the land and spoiling the new grass.

Gates

The best gate to use is the five-bar design, with a catch that is easy to open and close. It must be at least 1.4m (4ft 6in) wide and 1.5m (5ft) high – wide enough to allow the pony to pass through without risk of injury to his hips. The gate should always be chained and padlocked when you are not at field.

FOOD AND SHELTER

Every day, summer and winter, the pony must be visited to see that he has suffered no injury and that his shoes are well fitted. The farrier must trim the feet every month to six weeks and fit new shoes when necessary. Not all ponies need a full set of shoes – they may not need shoes at all. And, if the pony kicks, shoes can be dangerous. Be guided by the farrier. In winter, particular attention should be paid to a pony's feet especially when the ground is frozen as he is likely to bruise his soles and heels. It is dangerous and unkind to ride a pony when his feet need attention, so regular visits from the farrier are essential. It is important to check the paddock for holes in the fence and to make sure that it is free from all tins, plastic bags, pieces of glass or any other litter.

Dangerous plants

Many plants are poisonous to ponies. It is therefore essential that you learn to recognize them and keep the pasture free of them. Some are extremely pretty and it is, unfortunately, only too easy to dismiss them. Here you will see some illustrations of poisonous plants, shrubs and trees. Remember that, if they are found in a pony's paddock and eaten in quantity, they can be fatal.

Poisonous plants

These may be found in hedgerows or in the field itself. They are ragwort, deadly nightshade, foxgloves, hemlock, briony and lupin.

Poisonous shrubs

They often form part of a hedge. These are – privet, laurel and rhododendron.

Poisonous trees

Yew is extremely toxic and is fatal if eaten by ponies. The oak tree is not poisonous; however, its fruit the acorn is. The laburnum tree is poisonous if eaten.

Dangerous plants

Ragworth

Yew

Laburnum

Hemlock

White campion

Privet

Food supply

From April to July the majority of ponies will find sufficient food in the grass. In July, the grass begins to lose its natural goodness and, by October, it has stopped growing so its food value is not very high. In autumn and winter two short supplementary feeds made up of energy food – bran and grass nuts – and hay will be necessary. Ponies quickly lose condition if permanently grazed on the same piece of pasture without the land receiving some attention.

In spring and summer, with very small ponies, care must be taken to restrict the amount of very rich grass they can take. They can become too fat and may suffer from an ailment called *laminitis*, acute inflammation of the feet that causes intense pain. If the paddock has very rich grass, it is better to section it off with an electric fence, so that the pony is able to eat only a little at a time. The grass will last longer, and the pony will not overeat.

There must, of course, be a constant supply of fresh water, from a stream or drinking trough. Ponds are often unsuitable as they can become stagnant and unclean. In autumn and winter, the water supply will become frozen and leaves from nearby trees will fall into it. It is very important that the water is kept clean, leaves removed and the ice broken once or twice a day.

Worms

There is a high risk of worms in all ponies living at grass. The worms fall into four main categories: stomach bots, round worm, red worm and whip worm. If a pony has worms, he will lose condition rapidly. His stomach becomes swollen, and his coat will be *staring*, which means that it will be dull and lifeless. He may also suffer from occasional diarrhoea. If the pony has any of these conditions, it is important to consult a veterinary surgeon. In the case of worms, he will recommend suitable treatment. Prevention is the best cure, a good practice being to worm the pony every three months with a recommended powder from the vet.

Shelter

In winter, some form of shelter is necessary to protect the pony from the wind and rain. A shelter may be as simple as a high hedge or a group of trees. If no natural shelter is present, then a wooden one must be constructed. The best kind is three-sided, approximately 3.66m by 3.05m (12ft by 10ft) for one or two ponies and 9.14 by 3.05m (30ft by 10ft) for up to six ponies.

In summer, ponies are often worried by flies, and it is for this reason that a field shelter may be necessary. Again the shelter may be a natural one of hedge or trees, or constructed of wood.

HALTERS AND HEAD COLLARS

Halters and head collars are used to lead ponies and horses and to secure them when travelling and when they are being groomed. Head collars are usually made of leather and are very expensive. For ponies living in fields, a halter made of nylon or jute with rope is usually used. It is one complete unit with an adjustable noseband to fit each particular pony. To put on a halter:

1 Loosen the noseband.
2 Pass the free end of the rope over the pony's neck.
3 Adjust the noseband over the pony's muzzle.
4 Slip the top part of the halter over the ears.
5 Tie a knot on the left side to prevent the noseband from coming loose.

Leading a pony. The correct way to lead a pony and handle him around the stable yard is to hold the rope with the back of the controlling hand facing the front. Always wear gloves. A rope burn on your hand is very painful.

Running up is leading a pony, usually in trot, for inspection. When running up, run straight forward with the rope loose so that the pony can carry his head naturally. Always look straight ahead. If you look at the pony, he will probably stop or hang back.

A few diseases

Here are a few diseases that horses and ponies are liable to catch, but don't try to treat them yourself. If your pony shows any symptoms that you think may be serious, call in your vet at once. He or she is much better trained than you are to care for the animal.

DISEASE	SYMPTOM	DISEASE	SYMPTOM
Acne	Small boils and weeping sores	Lice	Irritation and loss of hair
Angleberries	Ulcerated and bleeding sores	Lockjaw	painful spasms
Ascariasis	Diarrhoea, colic and pneumonia	Mange	Scabs, intense irritation, loss of hair and thickening skin.
Autumn itching	Pimples and scars on legs		
Bilary fever	Fever, anaemia and jaundice	Oxyuriasis	Rubbing tail
Bot maggot	Gastritis and rectal bleeding	Pneumonia	Fever, difficult breathing
Brucelosis	Lameness and fistulous withers	Ringworm	Scabs which peal off to reveal ulcers
Broken wind	Heaves and coughing		
Ear mange	Head shaking, stamping and rubbing	Stable cough	Cough and nasal catarrh
Epidemic cough	Cough and fever	Strangles	Fever and nasal discharge
Glanders	Nasal catarrh, fever and pneumonia	Tapeworms	none
Leptospinosis	Fever, jaundice and pneumonia	Warts	Small, cornified growths

TURNING OUT AND CATCHING A PONY

When turning a pony out into a field you must ensure that the fencing is secure, that there is no rubbish in the field, that there is a good supply of water and that the gate is easy to open and secure. A pony is far less likely to consider getting out of his field if he has another pony with him.

Procedure

Fit a halter on the pony in the stable and, walking on his nearside (left), lead him to the field. It is a good idea to have a friend to open the gate wide for you. Lead the pony into the field, close the gate and then turn the pony's head towards the gate. Remove the halter and step backwards yourself, allowing the pony to be free. It is important once one has entered the field to turn the pony's head towards you as, very often, the pony is pleased to be out, may kick out for joy and could possibly injure you unintentionally.

Turning out is a fairly simple process. Catching can be more difficult as the pony is usually pleased to be out, enjoying the grass and will be reluctant to come into the stable. Try to gain his confidence with a little food or titbit given by hand. Remember that, if he is being fed by hand, you must keep your fingers flat lest the pony nibbles them by mistake. Speak to him softly. Do not rush or bustle. All hasty moves around the pony must be avoided. While the pony is eating the titbit, pass the halter rope round the pony's neck. As soon as you have positioned the rope, it should be possible to fit the rest of the halter.

A pony learns only by constant repetition and the association of ideas. A pony's brain must be calm and unafraid before he can understand anything new that is required of him. If you have difficulty catching a pony, it is a very good idea to visit him twice daily to give him a short feed or titbit and to make a fuss of him but not to catch him. In this way, he will begin to trust you and will come to you more easily and readily. It is foolish to enter a field with saddle and bridle in hand and expect your pony to be easily caught. Always leave your riding tack behind. Simply walk into the field with a titbit in your pocket and the halter in your hand behind your back.

Keeping ponies
at stables

Whether you own your own pony or help out at a stable you should understand that the life of a stabled pony is more artificial than that of a pony at grass. The pony lives in a *loose box* which should be 3.05m by 3.66m (10ft by 12ft). The bottom half of the half-doors must be at least 1.37m (4ft 6in) high, and they must be at least 1.2m (4ft) wide. Stable doors are designed to open outwards so that access may be gained quickly should a pony become *cast*. This means that the pony has rolled so that he is lying too close to the wall or door and cannot get up without assistance. Three latches are necessary, one on the top door and two on the lower door, one low and the other high. The floor must be hard-wearing non-slip and easy to maintain. The best type of floor is vitrified blue brick which can be found in some stables today, though blue bricks are expensive. Concrete is very much cheaper and widely used, but it is important to ensure that the top surface is always kept rough, and therefore non-slip. The stable must be free from draughts but well ventilated, with a good supply of fresh air. The best way to establish this is to leave the top door open. The stable floor needs bedding to encourage the pony to lie down.

Daily routine

All ponies thrive on a regular routine, especially a stabled pony who is very dependent on his groom. The pony must be looked over daily for any injury or loss of condition. A healthy pony will stand alert, with head up and ears pricked or more usually moving back and forth, eyes bright, skin supple and loose with a shiny coat. Normal temperature is 37.8 to 38.05°C (100°F to 100.5°F). If a loss of condition is noticed it is best to call the veterinary surgeon and follow his advice.

After checking that the pony is well and quartering him – that is seeing that there are no stable stains on him, cleaning his feet, brushing his front and hindquarters and laying his mane and tail – scrub out the water buckets and refill them with fresh, clean water. Now, the pony may be *mucked out*, see page 56. Next, he may be lightly groomed and have his feet picked out then have his first feed, left in peace and quiet on his own.

A pony must have an hour and a half after his feed before he may be ridden. Next, clear any droppings from the stable. Remove the rugs and tack up ready for daily exercise or work essential for stabled ponies. The difference between exercise and work is that the pony is *exercised* to condition him for the *work*, hacking, hunting, jumping or showing required of him.

After exercise, the pony is returned to the stable where his saddle and bridle are removed, and where he may wish to roll in his nice clean bed or perhaps take a drink of water. This is a good time to groom him, while his body is still warm and the pores of the skin are open, when it is possible to do the job so thoroughly that all grease and scurf are removed from his coat. Finally, put on a jute rug, untie him and leave him with a small net of hay.

There are always lots of morning jobs to be done in the stable yard, such as sweeping, cleaning tack or windows and stacking the muckheap. The pony should be given his second feed at about 12.00.

In the afternoon, the pony must be tied up again and any droppings must be removed from his stable. Remove any pebbles from his feet and make his bedding neat and tidy. Rugs must be readjusted and any extra blankets required for the night if the pony has been clipped out. Refill the water buckets. By 16.15, the pony will be ready for his third feed. Saddlery should be cleaned and the stitching checked. You may need to skep out again, that is remove any droppings from the stable, and fill up the water buckets. The pony may then have his fourth feed and also his hay net for the night.

The healthy, stable-kept pony is alert and kept in good condition.

Mucking out is the term used for cleaning the pony's bed. It is normally done early in the morning. The most common bedding is straw. A wheelbarrow, broom, fork, shovel, halter and head collar are necessary when mucking out.

First tie up the pony, take out the hay net and the water bucket, and then remove all the droppings that can be seen on the surface. Shake the straw with a four-pronged fork. Start at the door, throwing the clean straw to the side of the box. The shaking should cause the wet and heavier soiled straw to fall through the prongs of the fork.

It is essential that the floor is swept clean every day and washed with a solution of disinfectant once a week. It is bad for a pony to stand on a floor without a bed, because he may slip when turning, and will be unable to lie down when he needs to rest. Even more important, many ponies will not

stale, that is produce droppings, unless they have something soft, such as straw or grass, under them. When the mucking out is finished, the bed must therefore be put down again.

It is perfectly all right for the pony to have a thin bed during the day, with more straw added later to make a thick bed during the night. To bed-down, shake the straw well and add more straw as necessary. The bed should be deep in the middle with good banks around the sides.

Sometimes ponies are bedded on wood shavings which make very good bedding and are easy to keep clean and to handle. The procedure is first to collect a *skep* (basket used for collecting droppings), a fork, and a rake. Next tie up the pony, remove all droppings and wet patches with a fork putting them into the skep or a barrow, rake the sides to the middle and put more sawdust on top.

A well -mucked out stable.

Always shake the straw thoroughly.

Old cement bags make adequate skeps.

The stable yard should be kept as clean as possible.

55

Clipping

In winter, most ponies grow very thick coats. Depending on the work they do, some ponies need to be clipped to maintain their condition. This is a skilled job. There are four main types of clip. *All out* is done with ponies that grow very heavy coats, which are clipped short all over. A clip where hair is left on the legs and saddle patch is called the *hunter*. The *blanket* clip is very suitable for a stable pony, leaving the hair across the back, so that the pony looks as though he is wearing a blanket. A *low trace* clip is excellent for ponies who have to work and also live out in winter. Provided they are given a New Zealand rug to wear, they should be perfectly warm.

It is important to realize that clipping removes a pony's own natural blanket. At rest in his stable, he must have a substitute jute rug and, in very cold weather, one or two blankets to go underneath the jute rug. When he is working the pony will keep warm without a rug. At other times, if he is allowed to get cold and shiver, he will lose condition.

Many ponies will not need clipping. The thick coat will be shed naturally in the spring.

Feeding and diet

Feeding a stabled pony properly to maintain his condition is something that an inexperienced person should not try to do without guidance from a knowledgeable horsemaster. The pony has a very small stomach and, when at grass, he eats in small quantities but often. It is important with a stabled pony to try and follow this same principle as far as possible. It is preferable to feed him four times a day at the same times. In the feeding of all ponies, both at grass and stabled, the quantities and type of food given must depend upon the work required of him, the ability of the rider and the temperament of the pony.

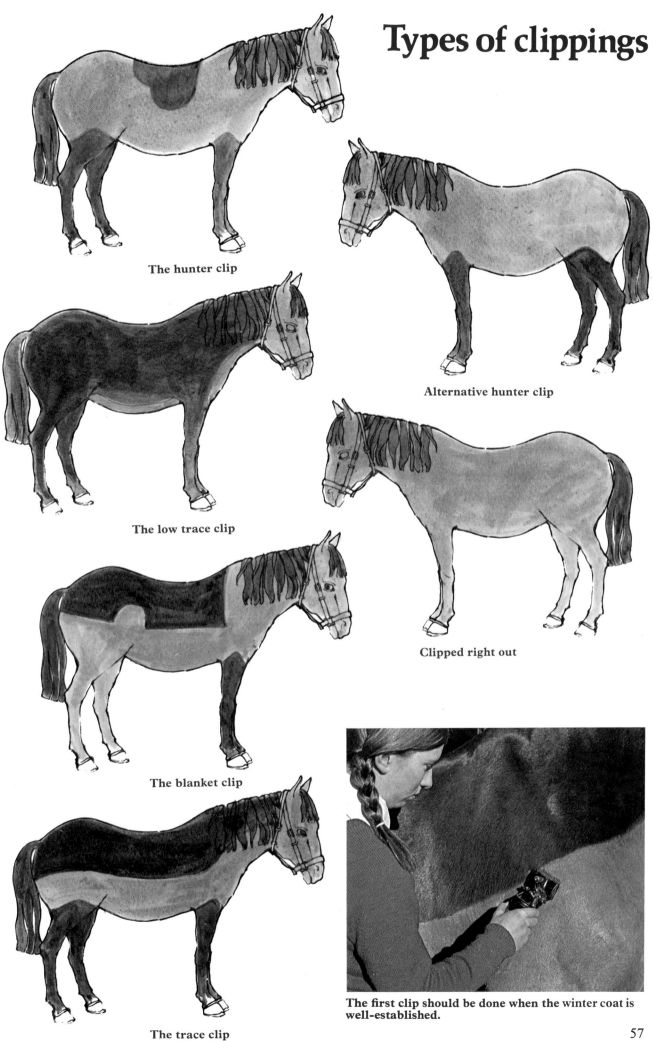

Types of clippings

The hunter clip

Alternative hunter clip

The low trace clip

Clipped right out

The blanket clip

The first clip should be done when the winter coat is well-established.

The trace clip

57

Chapter 5

Jumping and showing

One thing that all young riders want to do is to jump their ponies over fences, poles and hedges. Jumping is a team effort between pony and rider and there are certain techniques that you must learn before you start.

When ponies jump free they move very fluently with tremendous ease using their heads and necks to help them balance the rest of their bodies. If you understand what actually happens you will see why you have to adopt a different position in the saddle when jumping from that used when riding on the flat. The jumping position is supple and well-balanced and enables you to follow the movement of the pony without risk of hurting the pony's mouth. The jumping position is forward with you taking your weight on to your knees. First, you must shorten your stirrup leathers one or two holes to allow your weight to be taken on your knee and down into the stirrup irons. The angle between your shoulder, hip and knee should then be closed. Always keep your head up and look forward in the direction you wish to travel. Your hands must go forward and down on either side of the pony's neck so that he has freedom of head and neck to balance the rest of his body. If you watch ponies jumping free, you will see that the pony extends his neck and head out in front of him *before* his forelegs leave the ground, while adjusting his stride to jump.

There are five main phases of a jump:

The approach is very important. This is the time during which the pony is moving towards the jump, seeing the fence and gauging its height and spread. You must have the pony moving forward energetically on the correct lead, which will be your left leg on a curve to the left and your right leg on a curve to the right. The pony must be lightly controlled between your hand and leg, ridden positively at the fence.

The take-off. Here and just before the take-off, your legs are used actively to create more energy, should there be any sign of a refusal. Your hands must maintain a light but firm contact on the pony's mouth, ready to give and follow as soon as the pony is in the air.

The period of suspension. When the pony is in the air you should sit still in a forward position with head up and your lower leg encasing the barrel of the pony, giving him confidence and helping him to achieve a balanced landing.

The landing. Now it is important to keep your head up, looking forward, and allow your hands to follow the movement. In the *recovery strides*, remember to sit tall, keeping your legs firmly round the pony's barrel and using your back, legs and seat to help the pony continue forward with energetic and balanced strides. It is during the recovery strides that you must look forward and prepare the pony for the next fence.

Working over poles

This is the best way to begin jumping for you and the horse or pony. Poles on the ground are an excellent way to encourage the pony to loosen his back and to help him to strengthen the correct muscles for jumping. They will encourage him to put his head down and look where he is going.

Start with one pole, riding the pony at the walk on a long rein so that he quickly learns that poles do not mean anything exciting and that is part of his ordinary work. While walking over a single pole, it is a good idea to practise your own position, riding with a shorter stirrup leather and adopting the forward jumping position. If your pony will walk quietly and without any fuss over one pole, then try riding him over three poles. A pony of 14.2 hands will need the poles spaced about one metre (3ft 3in) apart for walk. With three poles, ride your pony actively forward with plenty of impulsion, keeping your head up and

Working over poles strengthens the pony's muscles.

Semi-circle

Riding a semi-circle encourages suppleness.

your hands and heels down.

When both of you can walk over the three poles without loss of balance or rhythm, you are both ready to progress to trot. Re-position the poles at a comfortable distance. Three poles arranged at a trotting distance for a 14.2 hands pony should be approximately 1.3m (4ft 3in) apart. At the trot you will find the pony is much more bouncy and elevated. Indeed, to start with the poles may give such a bouncy trot that you may find it difficult to maintain your balance. It is best to ride first in sitting trot, holding the neckstrap to help you keep in balance with your pony. Do this several times until you feel that you can keep your balance and your pony works at an even trot.

When you feel confident at the trot on both reins over the poles you are ready to ride over them at the rising trot. It is better to use a slightly shorter stirrup leather, so that your weight may go through your knee deep into your heel. Think of your hip, knee and ankle joints as hinges which will always open and close. This is what is

required of you to establish a supple jumping seat as these three main joints will absorb the shock you experience when jumping. You usually bend your knees when skipping with a rope and this is what you should do when jumping – bend your hip, knee and ankle.

When the trot is well established, begin practising the jumping position at the trot. The forward position must be developed so well that you can maintain the jumping position at the trot without loss of balance or rhythm. At first, it will be necessary to hold the neckstrap. As soon as you feel secure, you must practise without holding on.

To begin with, it is best to use rustic poles which are jump rails with the tree bark still on. There are two reasons for this. First, at the beginning, it is unlikely that you will be able to maintain your new position and keep a regular rhythm. If the walk and trot are a little irreguar, it is most likely that the pony will knock the rails. This will not matter if they are unpainted. Also, ponies often walk and trot better over rustic rails

than coloured ones because there is no glare to make the pony nervous of them. He will usually go over rustic poles confidently from the beginning. Nevertheless, before real jumping begins, both you and the pony must get used to working over coloured poles.

Begin with one pole on the ground, riding first at the walk and then at the trot. Gradually introduce two more poles so that the pony has to trot over three. The distance will be the same as the rustic poles 1.3m (4ft 3in) apart, and the poles themselves need to be between 3 and 3.5m (about 10 and 12ft) long.

Variations may be introduced as soon as you and your pony are able to trot over three poles on the ground in a straight line. This makes the work more interesting and will also help you to establish a more secure position in the saddle. You may now arrange as many as six poles on the ground all positioned in a straight line at 1.3m apart. Begin first by riding in the manège at rising trot and then as you approach the poles, adopt the forward

A low spread

The approach must be straight and calm.

With the hands well down, lift your weight out of the saddle as the horse leaves the ground.

Maintain a light contact with the mouth.

As the horse lands, regain contact with the saddle.

position, keeping your head up, knees bent, hands forward and low. With six poles the pony should go no faster, but simply lower his head over the poles and gain momentum slightly, still keeping the regularity of the pace. A good exercise to help you to become more supple and develop fluid balance is first to go over the poles in rising trot, then continue round and go over the poles in the forward position. Lastly, put the two exercises together by going large around the school on rising trot and, on approaching the poles, cease rising and sit still, so that you can use your back and seat to adjust the pace if necessary. As you canter over the poles, adopt the jumping position and, after the poles, return to riding in rising trot. You will thus be practising the main aspects of riding in a jumping position: the upright position for the approach, the forward position for the flight, in this case the poles, and the upright position for the recovery.

Another good exercise is to arrange the poles in a circle. This is excellent for keeping the pony

alert and helps him to become more supple through the curve. For you it is a good introduction to jumping, testing balance and security, because it is much more difficult to stay in good balance and harmony with the pony on a circle than on a straight line. Riding on the circle, try to keep your head up and look forward in the direction of the curve with your hands forward and low. If you experience difficulty in maintaining balance on the circle, hold the neckstrap to avoid hurting the pony's mouth.

Early jumping and jumps

As soon as you and your pony are confident over the trotting poles, and you can maintain a forward position in trot and canter, you are ready to start jumping. Arrange to have some lessons from your instructor who will help you establish the correct position. The pony should be a kind and willing jumper, and not too excitable or fast. To begin with, a neckstrap will probably be fitted for you to hold, so that you feel secure without catching the pony in the mouth if he makes an awkward jump.

When you are ready to start jumping, warm up the pony over the trotting poles. This will put him in the mood for jumping and give you a further opportunity to practise your position. Work over the poles two or three times and then give your pony a short rest. Next, arrange a cross poles fence 2.75m (9ft) from the last trotting pole. The cross will allow and encourage the pony to jump straight through the centre of the fence. Begin in trot and take the forward position for jumping, stirrups short, knees bent, heels down, head up and hands forward and low. Ride around the manège in trot, look beyond the fence and trot over the poles and the little jump. Remember to keep your head up on landing so you do not lose your balance. Do this exercise several times on that rein, and then arrange the fence so you practise it on the other rein. To begin with, you will find jumping quite tiring and strenuous. Ten minutes' practice each session is ample.

When you are able to maintain good balance over the trotting poles and small fence, you may progress to canter. In canter, you will not require the poles on the ground used in trot. Start with one very simple fence, keeping first jumps low so that you do not sicken the pony or unnerve yourself. A single pole approximately 0.3m (1ft) high on jump stands is an excellent arrangement. If your first lessons are in an indoor school or enclosed manège, it is best to arrange the jump close to the fence, to make it easy for you to ride straight at the jump with the fence providing a natural wing. Establish a good canter around the edge of the school. Keep your fingers into the neckstrap and look up, keeping your weight resting on your knees. In the approaching strides, remember to use your legs to urge the pony forward as you canter over the fence. A little work with poles and small jumps as part of your general riding lessons is a good idea. Specialist jumping lessons are not necessary at this point.

Single bar

The single bar fence is ideal for practice jumping.

Crosse poles

Try to jump the lowest point when jumping crosse poles.

Types of fences

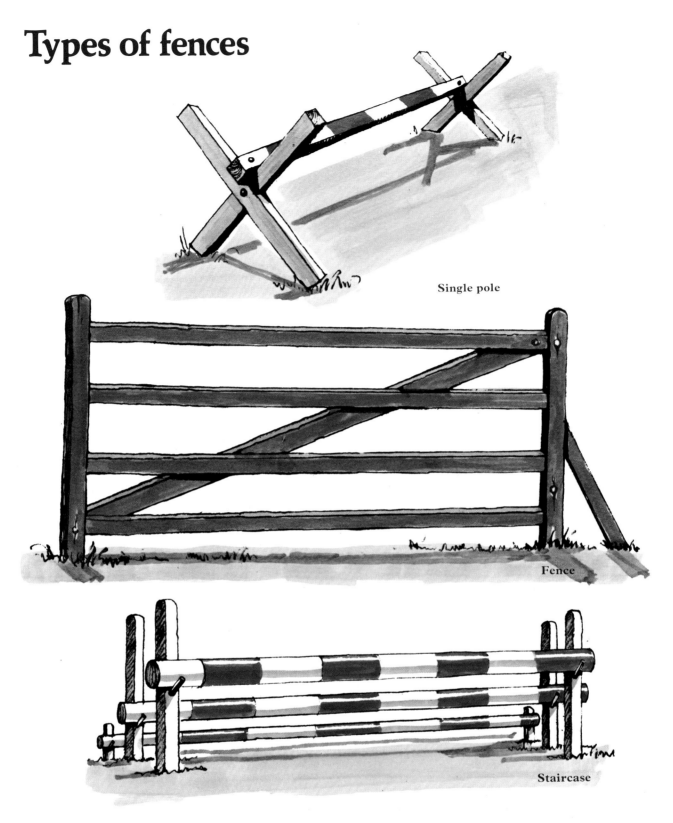

Single pole

Fence

Staircase

Types of fences

There are four main types of fence used for show jumping, the upright, the parallel, the staircase and the pyramid fence. The upright in a small competition may be a single pole, a little gate or perhaps a brush fence. The parallel is usually two poles of exactly the same height, in a small practice round probably 0.76 (2ft 6in) high and 0.6m (2ft) wide. The staircase is a gradual spread made up of three rails and a very inviting fence for the novice pony to jump. The pyramid, looked at from the side, forms a pyramid with a low rail on

each side and a higher rail, so that the fence may be jumped from both directions.

It is essential to start jumping on an experienced pony and to have an experienced instructor to help you. Never jump fences on your own without an adult to help you in case you should fall. Always wear a hard hat and fit your pony with a neckstrap to hold when jumping and assist in maintaining your balance. Losing balance when jumping is not only off-putting to the pony, causing him to make a mistake, it is also very easy for you to lose confidence.

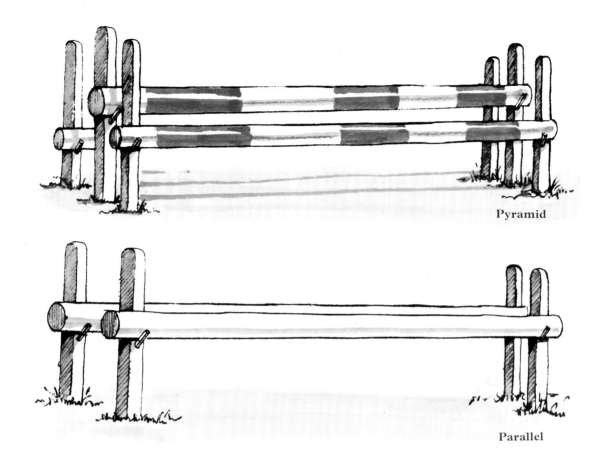

Pyramid

Parallel

Always have someone else with you when jumping – just in case of an accident.

H.R.H. Princess Anne trains for dressage.

What is dressage?

Dressage, to many young people, seems a rather boring and formal experience, because they do not really understand the full meaning of the word. Dressage is the step-by-step training of the pony aimed at making him obedient and supple so that he finds it easy to answer the rider's wishes. A pony with this kind of training will give a pleasant ride in countryside or competition. He will be able to turn, to stop and start smoothly, quickly and effortlessly.

In dressage, it is the rider's and instructor's aim to improve the basic paces of the pony when he is ridden. These paces should be regular and obedient.

Halt

The pony must be standing absolutely still on all four legs and fully attentive. The ears should flicker backwards and forwards, indicating that the pony is listening to you, the rider. He should be positioned to move forward from the lightest of aids you give. It is important that a light and even contact with the pony's mouth is maintained. All transitions, from halt to walk, to trot, to canter and from canter, to trot, to walk, to halt, must be smooth and well controlled, showing obedience to the aids.

Walk

There are three main types of walk; medium, collected and extended. In his early training, the pony will be asked to show only medium walk and sometimes free walk, when he is allowed to relax and walk freely on a loose rein. In medium walk, the pony should be seen to move with energetic strides in a regular rhythm showing four steps to one complete stride at walk. In free walk and medium walk, the pony nods his head up and down, while you follow the movement of head and neck, maintaining a light contact. In the collected walk the pony will be in a shortened form, with a more springy and elastic stride than at medium walk. The extended walk is the most difficult. The pony should calmly cover as much ground as possible, and maintain the regularity of the steps.

Trot

There are four types of trot; collected, working, medium and extended. Working trot is used in all preliminary and novice dressage tests and is the pace between collected and the longer strides of medium trot. It is the normal trot for young ponies and must be well established before medium or collected are achieved. At medium trot, the pony moves with a lot of power coming from the hindquarters. The strides are longer and cover the ground more than at working trot. At extended trot, as much ground as possible will be covered with a lengthened stride. The pony's stride is shortened, impulsive and energetic at collected trot, giving a rounded outline.

Canter

As with the trot there are four types of canter; collected, working, medium and extended. The length of the stride is shortest in the collected canter and longest in the extended canter. In the first dressage tests, the pony will be asked to show only the working and medium paces of trot and canter. Collected and extended are not asked for until the pony is much more advanced.

To make a pony respond to your wishes quickly and effortlessly and to make him supple and obedient, he should be trained to understand your leg and hand aids. Loops and serpentines will help to improve his response to the aids and make him more obedient. By working the pony on turns and circles and transitions you will begin to improve his balance, athletic ability and suppleness.

Balance is very important. Your pony will have been born with natural balance, but once he has a rider on his back this is lost and he has to readjust to carry the rider effortlessly. The best way to improve balance is to give a progressive course on the lunge, using a roller and specially designed side reins. The pony will be lunged on a circle using wide turns, until he can easily move away. When he lunges well, he should be ridden and begin work on transitions by increasing and decreasing the pace. Exercises to improve suppleness, such as work over trotting poles, will help to improve balance and athletic ability. In a pony schooled for dressage, what is looked for is one who works confidently and calmly, moving obediently forward, showing that he responds to the simplest possible aids. Training should not be looked upon as a means to dressage only, but to help the pony to jump better, using his limbs properly so they last longer and give you a better ride. He will be happier when he understands your signals and knows exactly what is required of him without being bullied.

If you are interested in taking up dressage you must be prepared to work hard to establish an independent seat. It is advisable to have help from a qualified instructor in some private lunge lessons, the best method of developing a deep and supple seat. This independence of seat is essential to apply and coordinate aids well.

Walk

In the walk, the four hoof beats should be regular and maintained in all work.

Reverse

During the reverse, the feet are raised and move back in diagonal pairs.

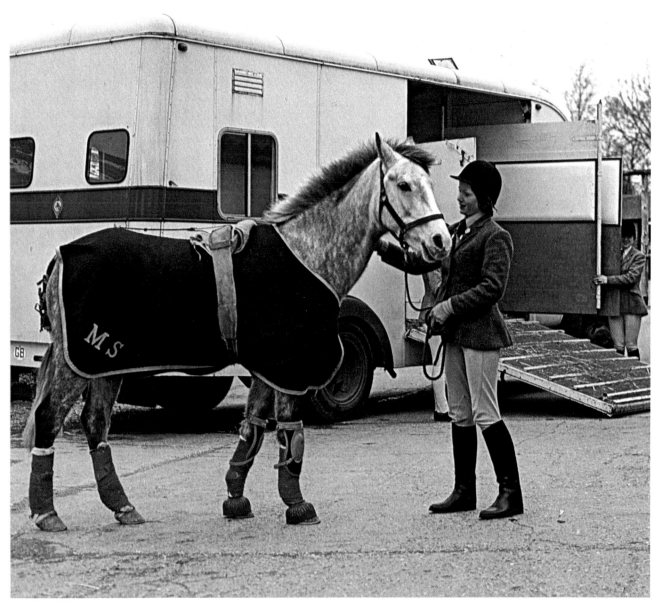

Travelling

Most ponies travel perfectly happily in a horse box or trailer, provided they are always handled sympathetically and driven slowly. Before loading, check that the box or trailer is in good order, that the lights and brakes work well, and the tyres are at the correct pressure. The floor must be bedded down with wood shavings or a straw bed. On a winter journey, the pony will need overreach boots, four stable bandages with gamgee underneath, a tail bandage, a tail guard, hock boots, knee boots, a woollen day rug plus roller and a halter or leather head collar. These give the pony warmth and protection. On a summer journey, the woollen day rug may be replaced by a linen summer sheet. Overreach boots prevent the pony from stepping on himself if he loses balance, perhaps when the driver has to brake unexpectedly. Stable bandages are fitted below the knee

and into the coronary band, passing over the fetlock joint. They give protection to the legs if the pony should knock or step on himself.

A tail bandage is an important item because a pony may rub his tail on a journey and make himself very sore. The tail bandage is also used to improve the shape of the tail after it has been pulled. It should never be left on for more than four hours at a time.

A tail guard also protects the tail and prevents the pony from rubbing it sore. Tail guards may be leather or woollen. Hock boots protect the hocks if the vehicle has to stop suddenly or if the pony fidgets a lot, kicking his hocks against the wall of the box. Hock boots are usually made of wool with leather fasteners. Knee boots, or knee caps as they are sometimes called, are essential to protect the knee from injury if the pony loses balance or falls while travelling. The top strap of the knee boot should be fitted firmly, the bottom strap loosely to allow full flexion of the knee.

A woollen day rug is worn on all journeys in winter. It is a smart rug and should be kept just for travelling and shows, a jute rug for warmth being used in the stable. In summer and warm weather, a summer sheet is sufficient. This is a rug made of linen or cotton which keeps the coat clean when travelling and is not used for warmth. Both rugs should always be used with a roller.

If the pony is to make only a short journey, for hunting, or a Pony Club rally, then it is perfectly all right for him to travel wearing his saddle and bridle with a rug on top. It is always best for the pony to wear the clothes described with a halter or head collar to keep tack clean for the ring when travelling to a show.

Travelling rug

LOADING PROCEDURE

Position the trailer or box close to a fence or hedge so that a natural wall is made on one side. Next make sure that there is clean bedding and that any equipment that you wish to take with you is already loaded. Looking straight ahead, walk the pony up the ramp and into the trailer or box. Do not tie the pony up straight away, but ask a friend to assist you by fastening the breeching straps or bar behind him, in case he should pull back and panic and rush backwards. If the pony is tied he will struggle and could injure himself.

Unloading procedure for trailer with rear unloading ramp.
1 Untie the pony
2 Take down the front bar
3 Undo the ramp and rear breeching straps
4 Quietly encourage the pony backwards

Unloading procedure for trailer with front unloading ramp.
1 Untie the pony
2 Put down the front ramp
3 Undo front bars
4 Lead pony quietly down the ramp
5 In a trailer with a large horse on the right hand side it will be necessary to swing the partition to make it easier for the horse's quarters to come round the corner.

Unloading in a horse box.
1 Untie the pony
2 Move partition
3 Turn pony's head and lead down the ramp.

Foam padding

Head Collar

Tail bandage

Roller rug

Tail guard

Over-reach boots

Hock boots

Bandage

A local show

If you own your pony or are able to hire one from a stable you may wish to enter a horse show. When you first visit the local horse show it is likely that you will be a little bewildered by all that is going on. Most shows, apart from the quite small ones, have two or three rings. To understand all the activities it is helpful to study a schedule, which may include any of the following.

Best turned out requires a tremendous amount of hard work on the part of the competitor. The ponies are not expected to canter or jump, so it is a competition that anyone may enter. The health and condition of the pony, cleanliness of the saddle and bridle, and the fit and good repair of the shoes are all examined. In addition the rider is judged on correct dress, cleanliness and general smartness. Such details as a tiepin and the soles of boots are inspected. In some classes, the Best Turned Out is divided into stable kept and grass kept ponies.

The working pony. This is a competition judged on the type of pony and his suitability for hunting, jumping and general activities. The working pony must have good conformation, be obedient and well-mannered, and will be asked to jump four or five rustic fences.

Leading rein classes. This is known as a Showing Class. The pony must be narrow, well-mannered and have good conformation. Leading rein ponies must be suitable for a small child being led by an adult.

The best rider competition is judged entirely on the ability of the rider. Any horse or pony is suitable for this competition. A well-mannered and obedient pony is most suitable, allowing you to ride at your best, showing good style. The conformation of the pony is not important. Best rider classes are usually very large and competition very strong. Competitors are not usually asked to jump, only to ride in walk, trot and canter on both reins and also to do their own individual show. In the individual show, riders will salute the judge and then begin their show, which includes a simple change of lead. This is a figure of eight at the canter, passing through trot and walk at the centre of the figure. They will then probably ride at gallop around the edge of the arena, pull up and halt. This shows their ability to control their mounts with the minimum of fuss.

Minimus jumping is a very basic competition over a low course, intended for young riders who have never been placed in any competition. The fences are usually about 0.685m (2ft 3in) high.

Novice jumping. Nearly all jumping competitions are graded on the experience of the pony and his previous winnings. This is an important point to bear in mind if, in the future, you wish to start competing. The inexperienced rider would be most unwise to start jumping in open competitions and, although one needs a pony who knows his job and will jump easily, he must still be eligible for novice competitions.

Open jumping is unrestricted. This means that any jumping pony, regardless of the amount of money he may have won previously, is still eligible to compete. In a small local show the open jumping class will probably be 0.99m (3ft 3in) in the first round. In larger competitions, it may be as much as 1.22m (4ft) for ponies or 1.37m (4ft 6in) for horses. When you are learning, it is a good idea to watch these classes and study the style and position in the saddle of the different riders jumping to improve your own position.

A well-turned out pony and rider.

A good take-off over the log in a novice competition.

Potato races are tremendous fun but require good horsemanship.

Gymkhana races. There are many competitions, such as trotting races, bending musical poles and potato races, which are tremendous fun. They require a really handy pony able to turn quickly, stop and start, and who does not mind unusual things such as buckets, flags and music.

The secret of success in gymkhana competition is practice. You must be able to vault on and off easily while the pony is standing still or on the move. The pony must also lead in hand, which

Slalom races require well-trained ponies and riders.

means that he must move freely at walk, trot or canter when led from the ground. Many ponies at first do not lead well and tend to hang back. You must not pull him or look at him, as this will make him pull back more. The best way to teach a pony to move well in hand is to position yourself close to his shoulder and allow him a loose rein. If he seems reluctant, ask a friend to encourage him forward from behind. Do not pull or chase him as he will be easily frightened. Reward him as soon as he understands by making a fuss of him. It is also a good idea to get him used to strange objects such as balloons, sacks, flags and buckets. If the basic training of the pony has been good, he should take to gymkhana work very easily.

Horse shows vary enormously in their size and organization. There is an atmosphere and tension built up among competitors that is infectious. You can become deeply involved in a show jumping competition or working pony class by pretending to be the judge, keeping the score and guessing the results. Of course, in show jumping, it is not so much a matter of guesswork as there is a definite, easily understood, scoring system. Four faults are given for knocking down a fence, three faults for refusing to jump a fence and three refusals will eliminate the competitor. In a showing competition, it is fun to select a pony you think will do well, and then see if your selection is placed by the judges.

Behind the scenes

To compete in show jumping, working pony classes, showing or hunter trials, you must be prepared to work hard. However good your pony, success will come only by working hard at home. Your pony must be obedient and will probably need some schooling to reach competition standard. If it is the first pony you have prepared for competition, go to a qualified instructor and seek advice, perhaps having a fortnightly private lesson to school your pony. Ask for a plan for the weeks in between lessons.

There are many horse shows in most counties. Select only those that are best for you, starting with the shows nearest your home to cut down transport costs and give you a reasonable idea of the progress that you are making. Send off for the schedules as they come out and begin to plan your season. All horse shows differ slightly, so read the schedules carefully, making sure that you understand the rules and taking care to enter yourself in the correct class. One general rule states that it is the competitor's responsibility to know the rules and not the organizer's.

For the ring your pony must be in good condition, with healthy coat and bright eyes, his coat clean and well-groomed, mane plaited, heels trimmed. The tail may be plaited or pulled. A good farrier is essential to ensure well-fitted shoes. Saddle and bridle must be clean, well-oiled and in excellent condition.

Good condition and a healthy coat come from the inside. Try to follow a regular routine, feeding the pony good quality forage at regular intervals, four times a day. If you suspect that your pony is losing condition or if you are worried in any way about the pony's health, do not hesitate to call the veterinary surgeon immediately.

Grooming. Thorough grooming is an essential part of daily routine. Keep your grooming kit clean. A dirty grooming kit will make the pony dirty.

Trimming. For a good appearance attention must be paid to the trimming of the pony's mane and tail. The mane is shortened and thinned with a mane and tail comb. The tail may be pulled and shaped at the top with fingers and thumb. Sometimes the tail will be rather ragged and the bottom is therefore usually 'banged'. To bang a tail the groom places a hand under the top of the dock so that the tail falls as it is usually carried, then with the free hand cuts the end of the tail straight across to a level with the pony's hocks.

Plaiting. For shows and special occasions the pony's mane and tail should be plaited. The object of this is to show off the neck and head of the pony to the best advantage. The number of

Preparing the pony for the show.

Plaiting

1. Dampen the mane.

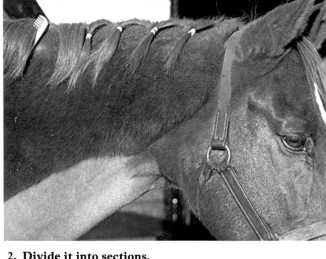

2. Divide it into sections.

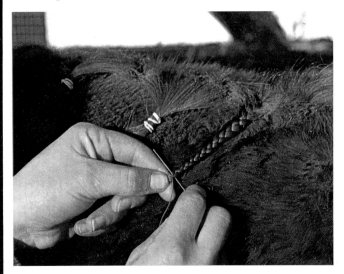

4. Pass a needle through the plait.

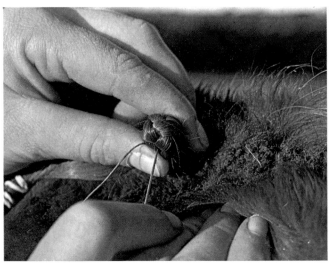

5. Wind the thread tightly round the plait.

plaits will depend on the length of the pony's neck: a short neck will look better with a lot of plaits and a long-necked pony will look better with fewer plaits. It is usual to have an odd number of plaits along the neck and one for the forelock.

Trimming the pony's heels, thinning the mane and tail, and plaiting all take quite a lot of practice if they are to be done well. It is best to watch an experienced person carry out these tasks and practise on your own pony several times before you attempt to get him ready for a show.

Shoes. The pony should be fitted with new shoes about a week before the competition, to get used to them. If by chance an accident occurs and the farrier may have nailed the pony's shoes on too tightly, this can be put right and any bruising dealt with in time.

Saddlery must fit the pony, be in good repair and safe. Avoid using coloured girth or reins, which are unsuitable for shows. Personal dress must be as neat as possible. The turnout of the rider is just as important as the pony's. It is well worth while saving up for well-cut clothes that really enhance your appearance on the pony and can be kept just for competitions so as not to spoil them.

Before the show
As far as possible, follow your usual routine the day before a show so your pony does not sense that anything special is going to happen. A suitable routine for the stable pony could begin at 06.00 with a check to make sure no injury has been suffered in the night. Tack the pony ready for exercise. He should have been properly groomed the night before so it is not necessary to groom him first thing. Give him about an hour's exercise, then return him to the stable. Muck out his bed and give him a fresh bed of straw, two buckets of clean water and a small feed. Remember to offer fresh water before the feed to avoid upsetting his digestive system and to prevent such ailments

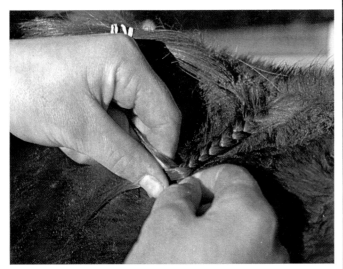

3. Plait tightly right to the root of the mane.

6. One finished plait.

as colic. There will not be time early in the morning to clean tack or the pony, the usual tasks after exercise. Most horse shows are on a Saturday, and the day before will probably be a normal school day. All this work must be done before breakfast. Exercising, feeding and mucking out should all be finished by 07.30. Leave your pony with a full hay net of about 5.4kg (12lb) and two buckets of water to keep him happy and contented while you are at school.

In the afternoon, when you get back from school, you will have a great deal of work to do, grooming, cleaning tack, getting the trailer or box ready for the journey. The pony must be given the complete grooming routine. The tack, saddle, bridle and girth, must be cleaned thoroughly though, if you have adopted the sensible routine of cleaning your saddlery every day, this should not be too lengthy or difficult a task the day before the show. The bridle must be taken completely to pieces and cleaned very thoroughly, the bits and buckles shined with metal polish, the leatherwork

cleaned in the usual way with saddle soap and warm water. The saddle must be similarly taken to pieces and cleaned. Such accessories as leather head collars, knee boots, and rugs should all be brushed, any metal work polished and the leather work soaped.

If your pony is doing a working pony class or a show jumping competition, he will have to wear studs, which come in many different shapes and sizes and are screwed into the outside edge of the pony's shoe. The farrier will fit the pony with special shoes with screw holes which are normally filled with cotton wool dipped in oil. The day before the show, remove the old cotton wool, and replace it with new pieces of oiled cotton wool. This will lubricate the hole and keep the area clean, so that the next day studs can be fitted immediately. Most ponies are naturally sure-footed and need only the small dome-shaped stud. These give the pony confidence when jumping and prevent him from slipping on wet or heavy going.

Having checked the pony's shoes, tack and cleanliness, it is advisable to check your transport. If it is hired transport, make sure the firm knows what time you are expecting them, the exact destination and how long you anticipate being away. If it is your own transport, make sure the vehicle has enough petrol, oil and water, the tyres are at the correct pressure, the lights and brakes are working properly and that the vehicle is properly licensed.

If you are under 17 years of age, you will no doubt be driven to shows by your parents or in hired transport. In that case, you need worry only about the actual contents of the box or trailer. Make sure there is a deep bed of straw, a first aid kit for horses and another for people, two buckets, a container full of fresh water, two hay nets full of good hay, one for the journey going and one for the return journey, a small feed of oats, bran and pony cubes, a grooming kit, Vaseline, anti-sweat rug, plaiting thread and scissors, hoof oil, fly spray and studs. A spare set of shoes is a good idea in case your pony should lose one at the show. At most shows there is a farrier present and, if you have the pony's correct size shoes with you, it is much easier to have a new shoe fitted.

The evening before the show it is sensible to get to bed as early as possible in preparation for an early start in the morning. Before going to bed check through your own personal clothing, putting your hat, jodhpurs, coat and clean shirt into a suitcase or polythene bag to keep clean. In the morning, wear your stable jeans, sweater and rubber boots so that your good clothes are not spoiled.

Try to arrive at the show at least two hours before your first event. This will give you time to groom the pony, ride him for half an hour and check your programme of events. This way both you and your pony will be settled and confident.

A likely winner of the best-turned-out event?

Tail grooming

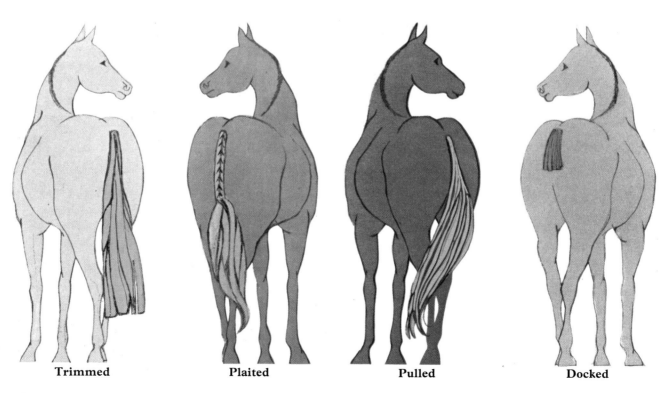

Trimmed   Plaited   Pulled   Docked

After the show

When all his competitions are finished, the pony should have his saddle and bridle removed and his rugs put on for his return journey. If he is rather warm, use a sweat rug with a cotton sheet on top, to cool and dry him. Offer him a drink of water and a small feed. After this, knee boots and tail bandage are fitted and the pony may be loaded into his box or trailer, where he should be given a net of hay.

Back at the stables, the pony should be put to bed as quickly as possible. He will be as tired as you, so the sooner he is stabled the better. Encourage him to stale. Remove travelling bandages and rugs, and check for injuries. The pony should then be groomed quickly, the feet picked out and any sweat marks or saddle patches remaining removed. Re-rug with a jute rug and give a bran mash with carrots or apples added. This is a laxative food, given because the pony should not work the next day. Finally, give him a large net of hay for the night.

The next day, go to the stable and check for health and injury. He must be led in hand so that signs of lameness and stiffness may be detected. Approach from the nearside and fit the bridle in the usual way. Take the reins over the pony's head and lead him out of the stable. Be careful not to pull him or look back. Try to encourage him to trot. Watch how he moves at trot to make sure he is sound and there are no signs of stiffness. Always turn the pony away from you, so that you do not get your toes trodden on or, if someone else is watching, you are not in the way. This means, if you are leading him on the left side, you will turn his head to the right so that you walk the farthest distance, not the pony.

As the day after a competition is a rest day the usual short feed must be reduced, and the bulk feed of hay increased. If the weather is fairly mild it is more pleasant for the pony to be turned out for a few hours, in which case hay will not be required during these hours. This saves on hay and gives the pony a chance to relax and have some succulent food. Do not make him go out in an unsuitable field. Check the fencing for safety and security, making sure there is a clean water supply and that the gate is properly locked. If your field has very rich grass, allow the pony out in it for only an hour at a time, or he may well gorge himself and perhaps give himself colic, a digestive disorder accompanied by severe stomach ache, or laminitis, a fever in the feet due to overheating of the blood and causing great pain and lameness. With both these ailments, the veterinary surgeon must be called immediately.

The show over, ponies and riders can relax.

Taking the water jump at a three-day event.

Advanced jumping

Before beginning more advanced jumping, it is important for the pony to be going in a relaxed manner and jumping in a correct style. For show jumping, accuracy is very important. The best way to improve is to work the pony over some gymnastic exercises.

Gymnastic jumping teaches the pony to be self-reliant and encourages him to jump in a relaxed manner. It makes it easier for you to sit correctly and allows concentration on position better than riding over big fences. Gymnastic jumping also improves your balance and sense of stride, helping you to find your way comfortably to the fence.

As the fences get bigger, style of jumping becomes more important. A pony jumps in good style when he approaches the fence calmly and straight. In flight, he should bend his forelegs together with the hock well bent and as close to his body as possible. He should use head and neck to balance his body, and his back should give a picture of roundness. To sum up, the pony should give an impression of ease and grace with minimum effort.

There is an ideal place in front of each jump for the pony to take off. You need to develop an eye for this place and learn to adjust the pony's stride by lengthening or shortening. A novice rider needs the guidance of a person who has a good eye and who is experienced in training ponies.

To jump over fences such as these takes a great deal of skill and patient training.

Jumping

1. **Look straight ahead to ensure a straight and calm approach.**

2. **As the pony leaves the ground lift the weight off the saddle.**

5. **As the pony begins to land, gradually regain contact with the saddle.**

6. **Try to keep a line from the pony's mouth through the hands to the elbow.**

Types of fence

Show jumps vary a great deal. As spectator or competitor, you will enjoy jumping more if you know what they are called.

Here are some of the types most commonly seen in show jumping.

Reverse Oxer

Upright of poles

A well-taken jump over a pyramid. Note that the pony's body is well-arched and forelegs are well tucked in. On landing, the rider comes back into the saddle ready to balance the horse for the first stride.

3. Lean forward and keep the head well up.

4. During flight take the weight on the thigh and ankle.

7. Try to land as smoothly as possible.

8. With the next jump in sight, control the pace and direction as in 1.

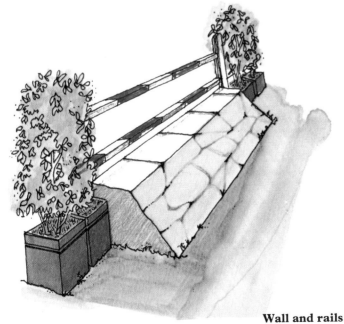

Wall and rails

Triple bar

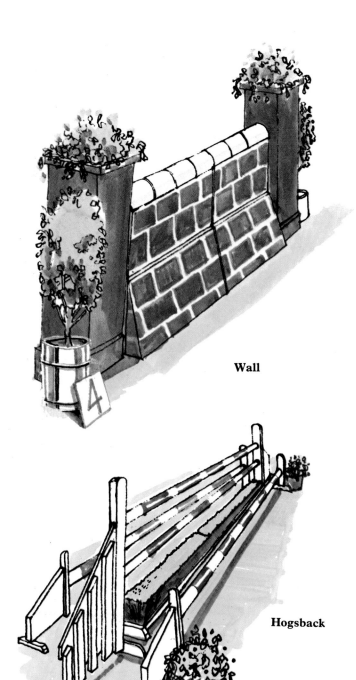

Wall

Hogsback

Water jump

Upright of planks

Rustic poles

Novice course

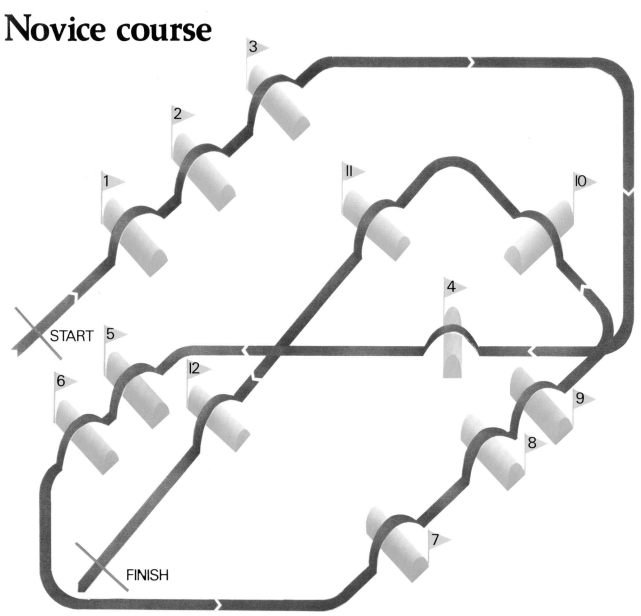

The course

Show jumping competitions are tremendous fun for spectator and competitor alike. The rules are simple. The style of rider and pony does not matter at all, as long as they get over without the pony refusing or knocking down a fence. The British Show Jumping Association (BSJA) and the Federation Equestrian International (FEI) lay down definite rules for each type of competition. It is the competitor's responsibility to know these rules and to understand them. Penalties are given as follows:

Knock down	4 faults
1st refusal to jump	3 faults
2nd refusal to jump	6 faults
3rd refusal to jump	elimination

If a competitor starts his round before the bell, this will also result in elimination.

Many faults occur as a result of badly ridden corners. If the pony does lose thrust at a corner, he becomes flat in his canter stride and will hollow his back and trail his hindlegs. Then, as he approaches the jump, he loses momentum and energy, with the result that he jumps flat and is likely to incur faults. Upright fences are more difficult for the pony than spreads, because it is difficult for him to gauge his take-off stride. The skilled and experienced riders will be seen to shorten the pony's stride prior to the take-off, as he needs to take off exactly in the right place if he is to clear the fence. Otherwise, he will probably get too close and hit the fence with his forelegs as he raises his forehand to clear the obstacle.

Competitors are always given the opportunity to walk the course before the competition to get a clear picture of the track as a whole. Walking the course is just as important for a novice rider in his first competition as it is for the well-known show jumper competing in open competition. First study the plan which is usually displayed by the collecting ring. This will put a picture of the design of the course in your mind before you walk it. Begin at the first fence, taking in its type, height and situation. The first fence is usually the smallest and most inviting fence. Very often because this fence appears small, the rider does not take sufficient care and faults are incurred.

Grand Prix course

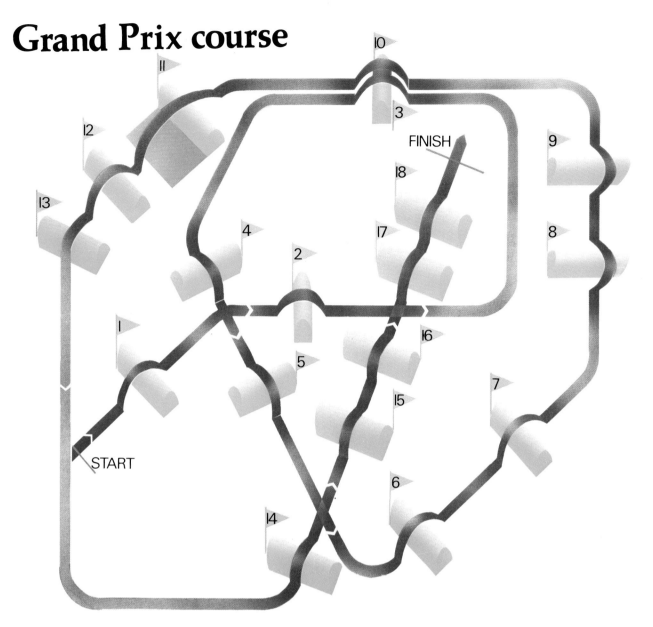

Remember to pace out the distances between combination fences, taking into account the types of fences used. Distances will vary according to whether it is an upright to a spread, a spread to an upright or a spread to a spread. A difficult combination is a parallel to an upright fence. The tendency is for the pony to jump in big over the first part so that he does not have room to lighten his forehand and put more weight on his hind-quarters to jump the upright out. This is why it is important to train the pony first over small fences put together to make gymnastic exercises, so that the pony can gain confidence to meet the bigger combinations in competition.

Show jumping is a popular sport throughout the world and television has made it even more popular. The fences in top competitions are sometimes as high as 1.5m (5ft). In fact, in junior competitions the course can go no higher, which is why they have become more intricate and complicated in their design. In open adult competitions the fences may exceed 1.5m, for example in a puissance (high jump) competition, the wall is usually over 2m (6ft) high.

Novice course
1. Start fence
2. Upright
3. Ascending spread
4. Gate
5/6 Combination of upright into ascending oxer
7. Upright of poles
8/9 Other combination parallel into upright
10. Gate
11. Spread
12. Wall

Grand prix course
1. Bruah and rails
2. Hog's back
3. Narrow stile
4. Narrow stile
5. Fancy gate
6. Treble triple bar parallel.
7. White gate
8/9 Double triple bar, planks and poles.
10. Narrow stile
11. Water jump
12/13 Double parallel bars
14. Oil drum and poles
15. Poles over a bank
16. Treble triple bar
17/18 Double oxer and stone wall

85

Chapter 6

Horses and ponies

If you decide that you would like a pony of your own there are many different breeds to choose from. On the following pages we look at some of the many types of ponies (and horses) that there are around the world.

Throughout the world there are many different types of horses and ponies. Many are easy to spot but others are more difficult to recognize as a particular breed. Over the years, however, in order to develop the best possible type of horse or pony for show-jumping, hunting, dressage, showing, and racing many experts have cross-bred in order to produce a horse or pony best suited to the work required of him.

Different ponies can be of many different colours. Certain individual breeds may always produce particular colours. For example, the Exmoor pony is nearly always brown or bay. The Shetland, on the other hand, may be of any colour, including skewbald or piebald. The colour does not affect the performance of a pony in

87

The Morgan

The Suffolk

The Arab

any way. It is helpful to know the different colours, because it is so much easier to describe a pony as bay than to explain that he has a brown body with black mane and tail.

SHIRES

These horses originate as their name suggests from the counties, or shires of Lincoln and Cambridge, Huntingdon, Northampton, Leicester, Nottingham, Derby, Norfolk and Stafford in the United Kingdom. In recent years they have also been bred in the south of England. The Shire horse is a magnificent horse standing 16.1–17.1 h.h. with plenty of bone. They grow long coats and long soft hair (feathers) from below the knee and the hocks and over the coronary band. They are not normally used as riding horses, but more often used to work on the farm and as driving horses pulling a cart. They have been used with great success in cross-breeding to produce hunters and jumpers.

THE SUFFOLK HORSE

Originally named the Suffolk Punch, these horses are widely used in farming in Britain as they have the strength and power of the Shire horse coupled with a little more speed and agility. They stand approximately 16.2 h.h. and should have well developedshoulders and quarters on rather short legs with good strong feet. They are normally active by nature and should therefore produce well-balanced movement in all paces. Their great strength allows them to be suitable both as driving and riding horse. They are also often used in cross-breeding.

THE CLYDESDALE

This breed of cart-horse originated in Scotland. Clydesdales are heavy horses with great strength for pulling and carrying weight. This breed is sometimes crossed with the Shires in order to maintain the size and the weight carrying capacity.

THE CLEVELAND BAY

These grand horses originate in Yorkshire. In their early days they were used widely for agriculture, being strong horses with powerful shoulders and clean, featherless limbs. In recent years they have been used for light harness work and also have been very successfully cross-bred with the thoroughbred to make good hunters and jumpers. They normally stand approximately 16.1 h.h. and are always bay in colour.

THE AUSTRALIAN WALER

This is a little horse standing approximately 15 h.h.; a cross between the thoroughbred and a cob. It is a strong, hardy horse and because of its sure footedness and speed is used widely in the cattle industry to round up cattle.

STANDARD BRED

The Standard Bred of America is a cross between the American thoroughbred and other, more sturdy breeds. The result is a horse standing approximately the same height as the thoroughbred but with more substance and heavier bones.

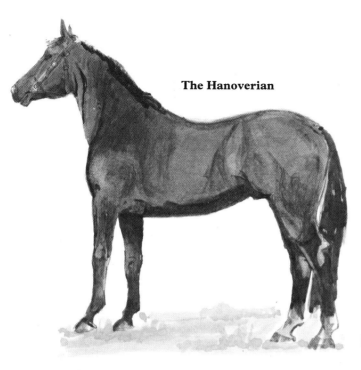

The Hanoverian

Percheron

The Australian Waler

THE AMERICAN QUARTER HORSE

The Quarter Horse stands no more than 15.2 h.h. and is sturdy in build. They were originally used in the United States for racing over quarter mile distances. They are sometimes known as 'cutting horses'. This name was made popular by the cowboys who used the quarter horse for 'cutting', that is separating individual cattle from the rest of the herd.

THE MORGAN HORSE

These delightful little American horses normally stand about 14–14.2 h.h. and are very good riding ponies suitable for adults or children.

THE APPALOOSA

Appaloosas are American spotted horses usually white in colour with black or brown spots. They are often used in the circus or show-ring and are well balanced rides suitable for all riding activities.

PERCHERON

These French horses are primarily used for agriculture and stand 16–16.2 h.h. They are usually grey in colour with exceptionally strong bones.

THE ANGLO-ARAB

This cross-breed between thoroughbred and Arab originated in France. It is a lovely combination giving the fine features and small head of the Arab with the added height and bigger frame of the thoroughbred. Anglo-Arabs make pleasant rides and have proved very successful both in the field of dressage and jumping.

THE ARAB

These are small horses usually standing 14–15 h.h. They are extremely hardy and are used with great success for long distance rides. Arabs as a breed have made a tremendous contribution to the horse world in that they are the original forefathers of the thoroughbred. Arabs are often used in cross-breeding, and have been crossed with great success particularly with the native British ponies. The main characteristics of Arabs are their small heads with 'dished' faces, and the way in which they carry their tails. They have very fine hair on both mane and tail and they usually carry their tails very high and sometimes a little to one side so that the hair flows elegantly behind them. Arabs are usually bay, brown, chestnut, or grey.

THE HANOVERIAN

In recent years Germany has become famous for the Hanoverian. Originally these horses were a fairly heavy breed and were used mainly for pulling carriages. In recent years more thoroughbred has been introduced to the breed and the result is a high quality half-breed with strong back and powerful hindquarters, standing approximately 16–17 h.h. These horses are now widely used for dressage and show-jumping.

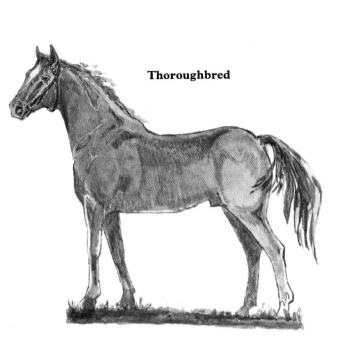
Thoroughbred

Dale Pony

Hunter

IRISH HORSES AND PONIES
The Irish are well-known for their ponies and horses for jumping, dressage and hunting. They are much lighter in build than the Heavy horses and are therefore not really suitable for farm work. There is no definite size or breed here. Many of the Irish horses are produced through cross-breeding from the thoroughbred using the hackney or their own native Connemara Pony.

THE THOROUGHBRED
Thoroughbred horses are the most sophisticated breed and are bred primarily for racing. Thoroughbreds usually stand approximately 16.1 h.h., are fine limbed with small feet, long legs and small heads. They are elegant and are bred for speed. They may be of any definite colour, although bays and browns are the most common.

THE HUNTER
Hunters are not a breed, but a type of horse. Their type is influenced by the sort of country which they are asked to hunt over. They may be thoroughbred or half-bred but they must have a fine sloping shoulder and bold outlook, be deep through the girth and be well-balanced to ride with a good length of rein. They must be able to gallop, jump, and pull up easily, and their manners therefore must be impeccable.

THE COB
Like hunters these are not a breed but a type of animal. Cobs are the working gentlemen, a handy and useful type who should give a pleasant day's hunting and carry weight. Cobs should be compact with fairly large bodies, short legs, small heads with quality, fairly short necks and good straight action. They must have immaculate manners.

THE SHOW HORSE OR PONY
Show horses are again not a breed but a definite type. Whether they are a child's pony, hack, or show hunter, they must have quality with 'presence'; personalities which are noticed the moment they enter the ring. They must be well-balanced with superb conformation. Their actions must be such that they move forward freely, calmly, obediently showing good straight action and elegant paces. Their manners must be such that they are well behaved under all circumstances. They may be of any definite colour but never two colours.

There are many different native breeds of pony which are suitable as riding ponies.

THE NEW FOREST
These are good riding ponies standing 13–14 h.h. and are usually bay or brown. They are extremely hardy ponies and are able to live out year round if they are given some supplementary feed in the winter to maintain their condition.

EXMOOR PONIES
These usually stand about 12.2 h.h. and make delightful rides as they are good to jump, despite their smallness. The Exmoor ponies are easily recognizable by their distinctive mealy nose and sometimes mealy underside to their stomach; they are usually dark brown in colour.

Highland Pony

Shetland Pony

Welsh Mountain Pony

DARTMOOR
Dartmoor ponies make delightful children's ponies and may be of any whole colour, black, brown or bay. They are often used in cross-breeding to produce children's small ponies.

WELSH MOUNTAIN
Welsh Mountain ponies do not exceed 12 h.h. and make the ideal first pony for a child. They are extremely pretty with a small, neat head and a slightly 'dished' (concave) face. They have wonderful temperaments and therefore are very suitable for small children to handle.

FELL PONIES
These are very strongly built ponies and are associated with the counties of Cumbria and Westmorland in the United Kingdom. Black, brown, bay or grey in colour, they stand 13–14 h.h. and usually have good clean joints and are well muscled in their shoulders and quarters. In winter time they grow a lot of hair and in particular are well known for the feathers (long hair) on their legs and also the thick mane they grow. They are suitable as riding or driving ponies.

THE DALE PONY
Strongly built and able to carry weight, these stand 14–14.2 h.h. They make very good utility ponies, able to be ridden by an adult or a child. Like the Fell pony they grow coats with feathers on their legs in winter time. These long coats protect them from the cold wind and rain, and in consequence they are able to live out without rugs all year round. As with all these mountain and moorland ponies it is essential that they receive some supplementary feed, such as hay, over the long winter months.

THE HIGHLAND PONY
These ponies originate from Scotland and are strong and powerful with short backs, well muscled shoulders and quarters, standing on short, strongly developed legs. Highland ponies may be as small as 12.2 h.h., but many are as large as 14.2 h.h. They make lovely rides, and are often used in trekking centres as they carry adult or child with equal ease. They are usually grey or dun in colour, although it is not uncommon to find browns and blacks. The greys and duns are easily distinguished by a black dorsal strip running from the wither to the dock.

THE CONNEMARA
These delightful ponies come from Ireland and stand between 13–14.2 h.h. They may be of any one colour although greys and duns are the most common. They have lovely temperaments and make ideal family ponies, being successful in many different spheres of riding such as dressage, show jumping, hunting, eventing and showing.

THE SHETLAND
These are the smallest of British breeds and stand no more than 10.2 h.h. They are strong ponies and are able to carry more weight than their height suggests. They are used as children's riding ponies and sometimes in light harness as well. These ponies can be found in any colour including piebald and skewbald, and have a lovely nature and will quickly become a family pet.

Holidays on horseback

The Pony Club movement is one of the largest youth organizations throughout the world and runs several holiday activities for members. The aim is to improve the standard of riding and horsemastership among young people. If you are interested in ponies and riding, you will benefit enormously and have tremendous fun as a member of the Pony Club. It is open to all young people under the age of 20 years. In 1976, there were 329 branches of the Pony Club in the United Kingdom and 1,053 branches in countries overseas. Each branch is self-contained, headed by a district commissioner and a local committee. This committee is responsible for organizing all the activities held by the branch.

One of the most important activities of the Pony Club is the working rally. There you will receive instruction in equitation and, when possible, in stable management. Very often at the beginning of a rally, the instructor in charge will have an inspection of tack, grooming and your own turn out, to improve standards of tack cleaning, grooming and dress. Of course, your clothes do not have to be expensive, but they do have to be clean and well-pressed, and a hard hat must be worn. Working rallies are the backbone of the Pony Club, where riders from eight years old upwards may receive help and guidance in all aspects of riding.

Pony Club tests and efficiency certificates are awarded to encourage members to take an interest in their work and training, both of themselves and their pony. The tests are D, C, B, H and A. D test is the first, a very simple test where the member has to show he or she is safe riding off the leading rein. Pony Club A is the highest branch award and requires a very high standard of horsemastership. Riders have to be 16 years or over to take the A test.

Most Pony Club activities take place in the Easter and summer holidays with some fixtures in the Christmas holidays. A popular activity in the Easter holiday is Pony Club hunter trials. Throughout the summer holiday, there is a full programme of working rallies, gymkhanas, one-day events, show jumping and the annual Pony Club camp.

Pony Club camp is usually the highlight of the year. In camp, you are taught how to care for the stabled pony, to groom, muck out, bed down, clean tack and to plait a mane and tail. Most Clubs take between 50 and 60 children to camp for one week or ten days at a time. The children are divided into groups of approximately eight to ten of similar riding ability and age, each group having its own instructor.

Pony trekking holidays are becoming more and more popular throughout the world. There are many centres in Canada, the USA, Scotland, Devon, Somerset and Wales, in well-chosen beauty spots. It does not matter if you are not a very good rider as trekking is very slow work, the ponies working in walk. The attraction is that you can cover far more country than by walking, and you can ride over rough ground, up hills and through streams where it would be impossible to take a car. Elaborate riding clothes are not essential. If you are a beginner, it is advisable to take some riding lessons beforehand at your local stables. Practise learning to mount and dismount correctly, to fit your stirrups to the correct length, and to put a saddle and bridle on properly. At many trekking centres, the riders are expected to

manage the basic care of their pony under the supervision of the trek leader. Trekking groups are usually 10 or 12 people, and the more efficient you are, the easier it will be for both yourself and your pony. If you are not very experienced, do not hesitate to try this type of holiday, but make sure there are properly cared-for ponies and experienced leaders. It is best to go to a centre approved by the Ponies of Britain or the Central Council of Physical Recreation. The British Horse Society is also able to recommend suitable centres.

Trail riding. These holiday courses are for the more experienced rider. Unlike trekking holidays, taken only at the walk, trail riding works at a faster pace, walk, trot and canter. It is essential to have had previous experience. Trail riding is always organized in parts of the world where the countryside is particularly beautiful.

A residential course at a riding centre. If you have had previous contact with horses or ponies and wish to learn more about stable management and riding, you may like to take a holiday at a riding centre. Many centres take young people for long or short courses, preparing them for competitions or refresher courses on general equitation. Courses vary enormously: some riding schools specialize in young riders, others in dressage, show jumping or general all-round courses. The best way to find out more is to write to your national horse society who will recommend the best establishments for your own individual interests.

Index

Page references in bold refer to illustrations

ACKNOWLEDGEMENTS
The publishers would like to thank the following organisations and individuals for their kind permission to reproduce the photographs in this book:

AFA Colour Library: 48, All-Sport (Don Morley): 5; Gerry Cranham: 2–3, 6–7, 12, 17, 20–1, 22 above left & right, below right, 23–33, 38, 42–45, 53, 54, 55 above left & right, below right, 56, 60–63, 68, 71 above, 76, 80–1; Bob Langrish: 40–1, 79 below left; Claire Leinbach: 1, 71 below, 82–3; Leo Mason: 79 below right; Jane Miller: 51, 77, 92–3; John Moss: 8, 11, 14, 15, 18, 19 above left & right, 22 below left, 39, 46–7, 55, below left, 57, 65, 66, 74, 75; Peter Roberts: 37, 58–9, 78, 79 above left & right; Spectrum: 70, 72–73.